D0328553

Our Darkest Hours

New York County Leadership & the COVID Pandemic

STEPHEN ACQUARIO
PETER GOLDEN
MARK LAVIGNE

Copyright © 2021 Stephen Acquario, Peter Golden, and Mark LaVigne.

All rights reserved. No part of this book may be used or reproduced by any means, graphic, electronic, or mechanical, including photocopying, recording, taping or by any information storage retrieval system without the written permission of the author except in the case of brief quotations embodied in critical articles and reviews.

This book is a work of non-fiction. Unless otherwise noted, the author and the publisher make no explicit guarantees as to the accuracy of the information contained in this book and in some cases, names of people and places have been altered to protect their privacy.

Archway Publishing books may be ordered through booksellers or by contacting:

Archway Publishing
1663 Liberty Drive
Bloomington, IN 47403
www.archwaypublishing.com
844-669-3957

Because of the dynamic nature of the Internet, any web addresses or links contained in this book may have changed since publication and may no longer be valid. The views expressed in this work are solely those of the author and do not necessarily reflect the views of the publisher, and the publisher hereby disclaims any responsibility for them.

Any people depicted in stock imagery provided by Getty Images are models, and such images are being used for illustrative purposes only. Certain stock imagery © Getty Images.

ISBN: 978-1-6657-0547-9 (sc)
ISBN: 978-1-6657-0549-3 (hc)
ISBN: 978-1-6657-0548-6 (e)

Library of Congress Control Number: 2021907194

Printed in the United States of America.

Archway Publishing rev. date: 6/8/2021

As the on-site incident commanders, you have to concern yourselves with the fear in your communities. You have to turn that fear into a strength and resolve of purpose. You have to act. You have to act and keep acting. That is the essence of bravery. And public service.

Stephen Acquario, Executive Director of the New York State Association of Counties

CONTENTS

Part 2: The Political and Public Policy Response to COVID-19

DEDICATION

This book is dedicated to the memories of all those we lost to the COVID-19 pandemic, and to their grieving families, friends, and neighbors.

Additionally, we dedicate this book to our county officials, who bravely served their communities in this most extraordinary time. These are the unsung heroes who put their lives on the line to serve us all, and they have our eternal gratitude.

Profits from the sale of this book will be donated to Feeding New York State, which supports the ten regional food banks that have been feeding the hardest hit New Yorkers.

PREFACE

By Stephen Acquario, Executive Director of the New York State Association of Counties

My mother needed appropriate personal protective equipment (PPE) and could not get it. It was the height of the pandemic, and she had been fighting stage 4 lung cancer for more than a year. She was receiving chemotherapy every Tuesday and Thursday.

Virginia Acquario was a vibrant and strong woman with two siblings, four sons, many grandchildren, and a loving husband. She was one of the toughest and most courageous people I'd ever known. She battled cancer relentlessly, and she wanted the PPE because she had no intention of dying from that virus.

A former nurse and the consummate caregiver of others, my mother turned her training to her illness. She researched constantly and sought every clinical trial she could. But COVID-19 took away most of those options, and she was forced to rely on telemedicine and twice weekly visits to the oncologist for her chemo.

COVID-19 kept me from spending time with my mother in the final months of her life. But we all did what we could. Every week, I dropped groceries off to my parents, and I worked with Dutchess County Commissioner of Emergency Operations Dana Smith to get the PPE for her, so she could go to her chemo appointments without fear of contracting the virus. My brothers also helped to ease her anxiety over the new, bizarre world of the pandemic, and my brother Adam was with her at the end.

My mother died on January 21, 2021. Her death was painful, and it was made more so because in her final days COVID-19 kept her from what she loved: time with the family, friends, and neighbors whom she had touched throughout her life. Worst of all, for me, I never had the chance to thank my mother for all she had done and how, by her example, she inspired me to dedicate my career to helping others.

As the executive director of the New York State Association of Counties, that is exactly what I continue to do, helping county leaders to make their communities and, by extension, the entire state stronger and safer for those who come after us.

That's the foundation of this book, which was commissioned by the New York State County Executives' Association (NYSCEA), an affiliate of the New York State Association of Counties (NYSAC). The NYSCEA is comprised of the eighteen county executives and the mayor of New York City. Together, NYSAC and NYSCEA are a product of nearly one hundred years of county officials working together.

The Association of Counties was started in 1925 by county officials who wanted to help each other and share best practices. It was a few short years after the Spanish influenza pandemic of 1918 and just before the Great Depression. These officials wanted to bring together all the counties of New York to teach each other what they were doing to run their governments and serve their residents.

I've come to really appreciate that early mission as I've witnessed our county leaders confront this COVID-19 pandemic. From the neighborhoods of New York City to the small towns in the Adirondacks to farming communities and suburban areas across the state, each area reflects its diverse populations. Yet from the onset of this pandemic, these differences did not prevent the county leaders from working together, regardless of political party. In 1925, county leaders came together to help serve the public, and that mission was still bringing county leaders together one hundred years later.

County leaders knew that what happened on Long Island and throughout New York City, Westchester, and Rockland counties would ultimately swing around to all parts of upstate. The tools used to combat this pandemic in the downstate region helped upstate counties prepare for it. And through the Association, all the county leaders helped each other do the best they could to prevent the spread of the virus.

Tioga County Chairwoman and NYSAC President-Elect Marte Sauerbrey said her county used the information shared through the Association to help drive the public health and safety decisions designed to protect their forty-eight thousand residents. Essex County Chairman Shaun Gilliland sought help setting up testing sites and wondered if they would have to turn the famous "Miracle on Ice" Olympic skating rink in Lake Placid into a morgue to store bodies. And Greene County quickly enacted emergency orders intended to protect its citizens and worked closely with NYSAC to share this with other counties and the governor's office in order to close sleepaway camps and schools with overnight accommodations.

At the start of the pandemic, we were sitting with Westchester County Chairman Ben Boykin in Washington, D.C., when he learned that Governor Andrew M. Cuomo had fenced off an entire neighborhood in Westchester to contain the state's first case. Boykin had to head home. The novel coronavirus had arrived, and his role as a county leader was forever changed.

* * *

By the end of March, over forty-nine thousand New Yorkers had died from complications from COVID-19. These were New Yorkers who lived in our boroughs, our neighborhoods, our counties. They had families and friends that grieved. And county leaders grieved with them.

At the state level, state leaders exercised expanded

executive powers over nearly every aspect of society, including hospitals and nursing homes. At the same time, they curtailed the powers of local governments, centralizing the response at the state level. Of the New Yorkers who died from COVID-19, thousands had been living in nursing homes. From the data, we knew that the long-term care setting was the most vulnerable. This data, which was not made public, would have helped state and local policy makers improve the healthcare delivery system. Politics and fear kept this data from being shared, a heartbreaking situation for the families that lost loved ones, and for the local leaders working so hard to protect them.

As the pandemic progressed into the late summer of 2020, we began talking about memorializing the actions that county leaders took during the pandemic to help stop the spread of the virus and to give those who come after us a firsthand account so they can benefit from voices of experience. By the fall, we had decided to move ahead with this book.

* * *

I am so proud of what our counties have done. I salute these local leaders for their fortitude and courage. Their task was trying, time consuming, and emotionally and physically draining. Yet they remained calm and answered the highest calling of public service. In fact, Onondaga County Executive Ryan McMahon lost his vision as a result of COVID-19 fatigue and stress. That epitomized the toll this pandemic took on county leaders.

Still, as we finished working on this book, the fight was not over. COVID-19 cases grew at the end of the year, and county leaders scrambled for vaccines to administer to their residents. That fight is still in progress.

Part one of this book tells the story of county leaders' experience in their own voices. It provides a glimpse into the fear, struggle, and pain they faced, and also the triumph they experienced in working to protect their residents—who were also their family, friends, and neighbors—from an insidious enemy. Part two provides a public policy account of the fractured pandemic response in the nation and New York State. It uncovers some of the many questions about which level of government was in charge of what parts of the response as well as how—and by whom—ever-changing policies were to be implemented and enforced.

The appendix is designed for researchers who want a roadmap for where to find more details about the congressional and state actions taken during the pandemic. It also provides key data on cases and deaths by county.

Finally, and most important, this book is about courage. The courage it took for county executives to lead and to protect their residents from the worst pandemic in one hundred years. Their public service should never be forgotten.

INTRODUCTION

By Matt Chase, Executive Director of the National Association of Counties

The pages that follow are the stories, by turns courageous and heartbreaking, of how county executives in New York State confronted the personal and financial earthquake created by the COVID-19 pandemic.

By virtue of my job as the CEO and executive director of National Association of Counties, I am the chief spokesperson for our country's thirty-six hundred counties, and I advocate for them with the White House, Congress, federal agencies, and the federal courts. The reason I find these stories so moving is not due to my work or that I'm familiar with the voices you will hear. Rather, it is because I am a small-town boy, and the lessons I took away from my boyhood have stayed with me.

In small towns, we tend to rely on and trust in each other. We cut and stack each other's firewood. We help snow blow each other's driveways. We hold our neighbors' mail while they're away. We watch each other's children. If, by chance, we do something wrong or simply make an innocent mistake, everyone knows. And there is no escape.

This is the circumscribed world of county executives. Many of them oversee counties with larger populations than the mayors of modest-sized cities. They are in politics, though it is not the noisy, cutthroat, ideological combat you encounter in the national media. County executives bear a more personal burden. Their idea of public service is that they serve the public, and nothing is more important to a county executive than the health and safety of their community.

This is not only the nature of the job, but it is because the people they lead are their neighbors and family. They see them at the supermarket or at Little League games. They live in the community they serve. Every decision becomes personal, and they have to earn respect and trust.

During the COVID-19 pandemic, county executives have seen their own staff, family, and neighbors become sick and die from the virus. I can't tell you how many county executives have spoken to me about the virtual funerals they attended. Sometimes, in the wake of these deaths, they express a sense of having let down their communities. Yet they wake up the next day, put aside their fear of failure, and focus on making their residents and communities safer.

It has been said that the government closest to the people governs best. I urge you to read these stories and discover the wisdom of that observation.

Part 1

The On-Site Incident Commanders: Local Leadership in their Own Voices

1

Dutchess County Executive Marcus Molinaro

"Dad's sick," my sister said.

Her phone call had come out of the blue. Since January 2020, I'd followed the news about COVID-19 as the virus swept across China and Europe. I realized it was a problem, but I believed—hoped is probably a better word—that there was a chance it wouldn't reach the United States. Yet even if the virus landed here, I had no idea how rapidly it would afflict us—at least not until cases began popping up in New York City. Simply going about my daily routine, saying hello to people on the street or at the office, I sensed how frightened everyone was becoming. A couple of weeks after New Year's Day, we started organizing our pandemic-response team and bracing for our first case. On a Sunday morning in March, we received a call from Ulster County Executive Patrick

Ryan. Pat said that his county's first case had come from a facility in Dutchess. COVID-19 had arrived.

And there I was, shortly afterward, listening to my sister recount our father's ordeal. Only days before, he had been fine. His symptoms developed slowly. He noticed that he was feeling sick, and then, suddenly, he collapsed. My conversation with my sister sounded as if a county executive was discussing the problem with a resident. However, as we spoke, the pandemic became personal to me, and it was hard to stop thinking about all of the families losing loved ones.

I did what I could for my father, contacting Westchester Medical Center and arranging for him to be admitted. I got a chance to speak with him for ten minutes before he went into the hospital. That was a blessing. I didn't know my father well. My parents divorced when I was young, and we had drifted apart. He started another family, and we didn't communicate again until the last several years, and even that contact had been limited to occasional texts or phone calls around the holidays. I had missed so much time with him. He never really got to know my wife and children, and the rare occasions we were together fishing or watching the Mets or singing Billy Joel songs became precious to me when I concluded that he might not leave the hospital, and this would be my last opportunity to make peace with our relationship.

My father went downhill at a terrifying speed. The doctors decided to put him on a ventilator, and it wasn't long before they informed me that it wouldn't be safe to take him off. Those two weeks remain a blur to me. I remember praying every day that I'd get five more minutes with my dad.

On April 9, a Friday, at 1:59 p.m., a nurse texted me to say that she thought my father didn't have much time left and asked if I wanted to call him.

I thought how strange it was, in this circumstance, not to be there in person, but I was anxious to speak with him.

The nurse held the phone to his ear. I told my father that I loved him and I wished we'd been able to talk about so many things. I promised that I'd stay close to my sisters, and that he should know that, despite the problems of years gone by, he was loved.

My father, Anthony Molinaro, died at 2:04. I am grateful that I got my five minutes.

* * *

County executives have myriad responsibilities, but perhaps the most important one will not be found in the law or our job description—to serve as cheerleaders for our constituents. Regardless of the challenge and how dispirited we might feel, we remain optimistic and emphasize the strengths and resilience of our community.

I believe this is always important, but never more so than during polarized political times and emergencies. The presidential election of 2020 and COVID-19 brought both, testing county executives and their communities in ways that had once been hard to imagine.

In Dutchess County, that first wave in March frightened people, and the common enemy of the virus brought everyone together. That was heartening. However, soon enough, the public became fatigued with masks and social distancing and the isolation. Some people were still fearful; others wanted to get back to living; some wanted lockdowns; others wanted us to open everything up. Residents who disagreed argued, and social media was a slugfest. We managed to hold it together because, at bottom, I believe, there was a willingness to accept that to beat COVID-19 we had to function as a community.

Generally, when things are going well, no one thinks much about the county executive. With the pandemic, I became a lifeline for community members. I tried to reassure them and answer their questions. I was worried about the impact of the pandemic on healthcare providers, and I did everything I could to support them, mainly making certain that they had enough equipment. There was such an intense emotional and physical strain on them, the stress of having to be engaged in so many life-and-death decisions. I wondered whether individuals would be able to continue going to work every day knowing they would face such a mountain of pain. But they did. And our essential workers showed a similar dedication. Their actions were performed under enormous pressure, not only the long hours they worked, but the threat of becoming infected. The frontline workers inspired ordinary citizens to help in new ways. Dutchess County saw massive increases in our Medical Reserve Corps, and many have volunteered to be contact tracers and help connect others with necessary services.

The heroism is easy to acknowledge and to celebrate. The losses are harder to discuss. The first loss was devastating, and the numbers kept going up. (By the last day of 2020, Dutchess County had lost 234 of our residents and had 12,018 infections.) Meanwhile, I wrestled with my grief as a son and a county leader. I thought of all the families who couldn't see loved ones in the hospitals and nursing homes, and it pulled at me. I wish that elected officials from the White House to the governors' mansions, to the cities and towns would appreciate the heartbreak of it. Too many people dismiss it, which is disgraceful and another casualty of the crisis. For every one of those individuals who is diagnosed, it is an hour or a minute that they are unable to communicate with a loved one. This has a devastating impact on the elderly in nursing homes and people with disabilities who are in residences. In my case, our daughter has a disability.

Trying to explain what COVID is and why we can't do certain things was challenging enough, but she sees Daddy going off to work and dealing with the related issues every day, and my wife and I can explain it to her. But what about those who aren't so lucky? Who live in isolation without understanding the pandemic? Hard to think about these souls, isn't it?

As shocking as the human cost of the pandemic was to me, I watched with mounting horror as businesses began to close, and I'm not talking only about money here. Long-standing community gathering places shut down and may never open again. Business owners and their employees, most of whom work hard to make ends meet, were left without an income and without knowing whether that situation would ever change. Savings and unemployment—even with federal help—won't last forever.

Fortunately, if there is one thing a county executive knows how to do, it is how to cope with the ins and outs of worrying about money. It's baked into the job description. What is necessary in our budget? How will taxes affect the community? Who will push for more spending? Who will argue for less? How many sleepless nights are in my future?

I knew that we were going to spend lots of money and weren't going to bring in enough to cover our costs. Now wasn't the time to worry about budgets. We would spend what was necessary. Building test sites and organizing transportation for those in need—to get food or go to the hospital or the test sites—wasn't going to be cheap. We had to think about whether the test sites would be in tents, heated or air-conditioned, and spaced for social distancing. We had to think about whether we had sufficient body bags and refrigerated cars for the rising death rate. Some areas were closing their homeless shelters; we expanded ours and opened up an additional temporary shelter. We took a vacant facility on the sheriff's office campus, creating temporary housing units with showers, medical capacity, beds, and recreational space. We let anyone who needed shelter come in. The risk was that we didn't know if somebody was going to walk in sick and spread the virus.

There have been other communities that haven't focused on the most vulnerable population—the homeless, the mentally ill, or those with other disabilities. That was their decision, and I don't criticize them. We took action quickly to ensure we were communicating with individuals with special needs. We coordinated with service providers via our rapid response team with regular weekly calls and directed personal protective equipment to help them, even when the state told us not to. That was tough. There were times when the state said that PPE must go to here, but not there, and we disagreed. We met our needs. Mental health went to the top of our list. Telemedicine, telepsychology, and teletherapy all became critical.

I think we made the right choices and reacted as well as one could expect. Gradually, though, I could feel the mounting financial pressure.

The loss of sales tax was going to be a disaster. As far as we knew when the year started, assessed valuation was going to be stable for 2020. We were going to get our property taxes. But the one thing we had no control over was the loss of the sales tax revenue. We were prepared for the worst. We estimated it could be as bad as a $75 million loss, and we did a little better, but this is still financially untenable. You don't have the luxury in government to back out of commitments. There are services we are legally required to provide, and the shortfall of revenue made it difficult to do this. Add that to the uncertainty of federal and state assistance, we are in the dark and still weathering that storm.

From the start, my biggest concern was the unknown. Would the cases continue to rise? Would we have to open more facilities? We were prepared to use Dutchess Community College as an auxiliary medical center. We were preparing it and asking ourselves if we'd have sufficient room. Or would we be fighting other counties for space?

We want to help everybody, but we also need to provide the resources and services to our own folks. Will the state demand that we move resources out of Dutchess and give it to other people? Will they force other patients to relocate into this community? All of that became so challenging and, at times, adversarial. That worried us every day. We never knew what Governor Andrew Cuomo would order us to do.

New York State decentralizes its public-health response, so in a pandemic, counties effectuate the policy. The governor can have a press conference and issue executive orders and order the State Health Department to do certain things, but it doesn't get done unless the counties do it. There is no flattening the curve or pandemic response without county governments, and there will be no rebuilding of our economy or overcoming any challenges of the pandemic without us. There are nineteen hundred public health departments administered by counties across the United States, but none of them function the way we do in New York. We succeed by having county-to-county relationships that encourage the act of picking up the phone and learning from others by listening and sharing information.

We have leaned on one another. It has defined our

success, but it also has meant that in the face of loss, we had each other as local officials. The fact that Ulster County had a new county executive who came to office with professional and military experience made his perspective invaluable to somebody like me. In turn, my twenty-five years of working in government was invaluable to him.

We try to please everybody all while knowing that we can't. We tried to provide a sense of security. We coordinated with service providers to feed and house people—with Dutchess Outreach to Mental Health America, Hudson River Housing, and other core providers. We just kept cutting checks because, God forbid, people would have no place to go if they were homeless or hungry or sick. And we are going to keep at it. We are grateful for everything we could do and will try to do more. We will grieve for those we lost. We will pray for the best and prepare for the worst.

And we will hope for a better tomorrow.

2

Albany County Executive Daniel McCoy

At the end of December 2019, after returning from a meeting in Washington, D.C., I felt sick. Winter in Albany is primetime for feeling rundown with cold symptoms, so I didn't think much of it until the spring when a doctor told me, following an antibody test, that somewhere between December and February, I'd been infected with COVID-19. In February, I'd gone to Texas for National Guard duty and to Maryland for a meeting; the next month, I'd been in New York City. To this day, I have no idea where or how I'd picked up the virus, but what I do know—and will never forget—is that on March 12, 2020, Albany County recorded its first two confirmed cases of COVID-19.

If there is one lesson I learned while working as a firefighter and EMT and serving in Iraq during 2005 and 2006, it is that when responding to a crisis, you don't always have time to plot out every strategy. All you can do is act quickly to save lives, and learn from your successes and mistakes.

First thing I did was recommend canceling the St. Patrick's Day Parade in Albany, and two days later I declared a state of emergency, which allowed the temporary modification of laws and regulations—for example, procurement policies—so we didn't waste any time responding to the virus. Then I redeployed county employees to deal with our new reality: information services arranged for us to operate remotely; our probation staff supported our health department to check on people under mandatory quarantine; over two hundred employees were trained in contact tracing and we had people looking in on our long-term care facilities. Normally, our department of health provides important services to our constituents, but sadly they sometimes go unappreciated. That changed when the virus showed up, and their vital role was on full display. With some health experts predicting that the virus could spiral out of control, we looked for ways to prevent hospitals from being overwhelmed. We did this in part by contacting hotel owners, and I was heartened to have quite a few of these businesses offer their hotels as potential housing for the sick or quarantined. We also partnered with St. Peter's Health Partners and made a separate wing of our nursing home available if hospitals needed extra beds. The wing has separate ventilation, entrances, and staffing from St. Peter's. When we struggled to procure personal protective equipment, we also enlisted the help of our business community. So many local companies literally changed the way they did business to provide us with life-saving supplies that we distributed to our hospitals, first responders, schools, and other essential workers.

* * *

One crucial aspect of our COVID-19 response was communicating with the public as well as my counterparts across the state and country. My daily press conferences were a great way to reassure people and to provide updates on how their lives would be changing. As the virus spread, I was joined by Albany County Department of Health Commissioner Dr. Elizabeth Whalen to provide guidance to the community. I used the press conferences to announce my concerns and to bring in the sheriff, district attorney, mayor, faith, business and school leaders to offer their expertise and insight. My office also functioned as a source of information for the public. My staff fielded calls, emails, and messages on social media related to the shutdown, local response activities, unemployment, reopening, general information, complaints, and more. Our administrative staff answered the questions they could and forwarded other questions to the appropriate staff for follow-up. And as president of both the County Executives of America as well as the NYS County Executives' Association, I have been able to share what we have learned with my colleagues and in turn, heard about their successes and challenges.

We were learning on the fly, and I'm especially proud of our food distribution program. By partnering with the Regional Food Bank of Northeastern New York and the National Guard, we were able to deliver fifty-six hundred boxes of food (each box contained around thirty-five pounds of groceries) to quarantined families in just over two months. The program enabled people to comply with quarantine orders and helped to depress the infection rate.

We were also able to launch mobile testing sites. I'd seen the reports showing that COVID-19 was disproportionately impacting Black and Brown communities, and the ability to partner with a trusted healthcare provider like Whitney M. Young, Jr. Health Center and bring testing directly to underserved communities was a source of pride for the county, and Albany County was one of the first in the state to do so. Locating the testing sites within minority and lower socioeconomic communities was crucial to monitoring infection rates and community spread among a vulnerable population.

It became clear early on that any extended economic shutdown and quarantine would have serious implications on the mental well-being of residents. That's why within the first week of us identifying our first positive cases, we established a mental health support line to help those struggling with anxiety, depression, or simply struggling to make sense of everything. We had experts on the phone reassuring people that they were never alone during this crisis. This had far-reaching benefits, and I count it as one of the most important actions we took during the worst of the pandemic.

Another inequity that we've improved on, yet still have work to do, is access to broadband. Far too many families in the Hilltowns, a rural section of the county, don't have reliable connectivity to the internet. This was a serious issue before the outbreak of COVID-19 as internet capabilities can determine your success as a business and the strength of an economy. But as schools were shuttered because of the virus and parents became de facto teachers at home, taking action couldn't wait. We partnered with Hudson Valley Wireless, which was able to utilize a cell tower on county property that allowed the service provider to reach more residents with children at the Berne-Knox-Westerlo School District.

* * *

In order to help people get back to work and to prevent residents from losing their businesses or their life savings, we supported the business community by helping them make sense of the state health guidelines and advocating for any of the businesses that were left out of the Phase 4 reopening. I understood that the state was attempting to keep the infection rate low, but we also needed to be fair to our malls, gyms, and movie theaters. We also managed to pass along the hand sanitizer acquired from the state.

The economic impact of the pandemic underscored the need to have a way—some sort of local infrastructure—to direct aid to small businesses that were unable to take advantage of federal stimulus programs. Industrial development agencies within Albany County were able to offer grants to private business, but a similar mechanism didn't exist at the county level. So COVID prompted my Economic Development team to lay the framework for a business response plan that would immediately be able to offer grants, not loans, during any future challenges.

* * *

Any response to a pandemic requires a partnership between state and local governments, and overall, we worked well with the State of New York. That isn't to say there weren't some speed bumps. County government workforces were already stretched thin dealing with the public health implications of the crises, but the governor's executive orders required us to shoulder an even greater workload. Here's one example: the state established the PAUSE Enforcement Assistance Task Force, where individuals could complain about the operation of nonessential businesses or gatherings. Yet the county had to assess the validity of the complaints and forward them to the appropriate law enforcement jurisdiction for follow-up.

At times, communication from the state wasn't as helpful as we'd hoped. When it came to shutdowns and reopening plans, the state left county governments scrambling to respond once updates were announced at the governor's briefings. The state has somewhat rectified the initial lack of communication by establishing regional control rooms. The rooms are an effective way to interact with officials, but they don't give control to local decision-makers. Furthermore, the governor's orders raised legal and jurisdictional questions which further complicated enforcement measures. This increased burden has taken a toll on our coffers. Yet the governor has been unwilling to share any of the money received from the Coronavirus Relief Fund, and this has left us grasping for a lifeline.

Finally, there have been discrepancies in the reporting of COVID-19 hospitalizations, cases, and deaths between the county and New York State. While the state was using Hospital Emergency Response Data System to count hospitalizations and deaths, we were using a more in-depth forensic accounting of deaths by verifying the residence of those who passed away. I argued that the state's data wasn't truly reflective of community level spread, because people were being sent to our hospitals from outside the county and the Capital Region.

* * *

When we begin to analyze what went well and what did not, what was truly important was the partnership among Albany County and other counties across the state and the country. That includes working with the New York State Association of Counties and Executive Director Steve Acquario, as well as the National Association of Counties CEO Matt Chase and County Executives of America

Executive Director Mike Griffin. I know how critical these organizations and their membership are. In these roles, I was able to help acquire personal protective equipment and direct it to some of the counties and regions that needed it most. And perhaps most important, by being able to share our own stories through countless phone calls, we avoided making unnecessary mistakes and pursued policies that had already been proven effective by our counterparts.

* * *

Time will tell us about the lasting impact of the crisis on our communities. For now, I can say that we've been hit hard. The Albany-Schenectady-Troy metro area lost roughly forty thousand jobs between September 2019 and 2020. When you have people losing wages, jobs, and businesses, the fallout is mind-numbing. Applications for the Supplemental Nutrition Assistance Program in our county have increased by over 35 percent between August 2019 and 2020. Statewide, the number of New Yorkers reporting food insecurity nearly doubled. And this financial uncertainty and social isolation can exacerbate mental health and addiction issues. Sadly, like numerous counties across the state, we've seen a surge in opioid overdose deaths—ninety-nine of our residents, up 60 percent over the same period last year. Social isolation is also taking a toll. The quarantine has worsened domestic violence, but because victims had to remain home, they felt less comfortable reporting abuse. A similar case can be made for child abuse and neglect. Without children going into classrooms, teachers are less able to uncover and report dangerous situations.

Eleven months have passed since our first cases. Currently, over nineteen thousand residents are positive for COVID-19, and 345 have died from it, a number that haunts me. Now, at least, the vaccine has arrived, and I hope the supply will increase to make it available to everyone. Still, it will be months before we outrun the pandemic, and one of my greatest concerns is COVID fatigue. Closing the economy and urging residents to stay home was a lot to ask of people. Businesses and individuals made incredible sacrifices. This may have been the price of preventing even more deaths. However, now people are anxious to get back to normal. As leaders, we need to preserve a careful balance between keeping people safe—encouraging them to continue to wear masks, maintain social distance, and wash their hands, while they are returning to their lives.

I am proud of what we managed to accomplish here. As for the future, one thing I can say for certain—like every step we took during the pandemic—we will learn as we go, doing all we can to protect and restore our county.

3

Broome County Executive Jason Garnar

When I became the county executive in 2017, a friend kidded me, saying, "You're the kind of executive who gets all the state of emergencies." Soon after, as if to prove his point, a storm dumped three feet of snow on us in twenty-four hours.

Yet nothing could have prepared me for COVID-19. It happened so fast. In February, we watched the virus from afar, and within a month, I declared a state of emergency. By then, we had established an emergency operations center, where my executive team met daily with people from our health department and office of emergency services. And I had to issue a number of orders, which, a few weeks before, would've seemed unthinkable—stopping buses from entering the county; preventing gatherings of large groups; establishing new rules for daycare; and closing the schools.

We needed our doctors, nurses, all our healthcare people, and the police, and a whole variety of essential employees, so we arranged daycare for their children, and because at least half the students in Broome County rely on the schools for food, we set up dozens of food distribution sites, and I think we distributed well over a million meals to kids in our community.

My biggest concern was that the virus would spread like wildfire and overwhelm our healthcare system. We brought in leaders from our hospitals, UHS Binghamton and Ascension Lourdes, and we decided to augment their available space by putting together a triage unit in the Broome County Veterans Memorial Arena with about fifty beds.

Hospital and nursing home administrators urged us to make sure that their staff had enough personal protective equipment. We've been through so much with the pandemic, it's hard to recall exactly what was going on eight or nine months ago, but we had major problems in the supply chain of PPE.

We have a lot of do-it-yourselfers here who do projects around their homes, and sometimes they have PPE lying around unopened in packages. I was doing daily briefings for the media then, and I remember announcing, "Residents of Broome County, your homework assignment is to go to your garage or your basement and see if you have any N95 masks."

We had a donation site, and the community really stepped up. I found a couple of N95 masks at my own house and donated them. A lot of people found gloves. This didn't solve our PPE shortage—ultimately there were state stockpiles that our hospitals and nursing homes could access—but watching people bring in donations was amazing. And it was empowering for them to actively fight against COVID-19.

My afternoon briefings were televised, and I heard numerous accounts from people in the community who said that they would tune in the governor around eleven or twelve, and at three they'd watch me for the local update. The briefing enabled me to talk about what had to be done to prevent the spread of the virus and to announce shutdowns, donation drives, mask distributions, anything I thought people needed to know. County employees did extensive mask distributions—at a mall and a park. Literally, thousands of people came in their cars, and I believe we distributed well over sixty thousand masks at those sites.

The business shutdowns were terrible for us—for those who lost their jobs and for the county's sales tax revenue. We knew there had to be a process for reopening them, but it was going to be a drastic one. We had them submit their plans, which included proper sanitization every day, the right PPE, and rules for social distancing. County executives in our region were having conversations with the state on a daily basis. We would ask and receive information we needed for phased reopenings. These talks gave me the opportunity to connect with county executives in my area. We could bounce ideas off each other as we went through the crisis and learned what had worked for each of us and what hadn't.

As the state started to roll out its phased-in reopening plan, we were at the top of the list because our infection rate was low. The plan was complex—Phase 1, Phase 2, Phase 3, Phase 4—and it was being applied to all different types of businesses and industries, so naturally the people running these places had no shortage of questions about how to comply. I assigned a fair amount of my staff to do nothing but dispense information and respond to the hundreds, if not thousands, of phone calls, emails, and Facebook messages that we received. We also conducted several Zoom meetings with our local businesses, and each meeting drew hundreds of participants eager to be educated about the ins and outs of reopening that we were hearing from the state.

We were able to reopen our economy in a way that was safe. Good thing, too, because the business community was suffering. Prior to the pandemic, our unemployment rate was 4 percent. In the first few months after COVID-19 got here, the rate jumped to 15 percent. We are now at 5.5 percent. While this is a testament to our ability to work with businesses, I look at numbers and remind myself that I am looking not at a graph, but at the lives of individuals and their families. Yes, the numbers have improved, but not enough for me.

Our health department established liaisons with our public and private schools, our community college, and Binghamton University. That way, during reopenings, their questions could be answered. There was a good deal of work the schools needed to do in order to reopen, and they received support from the county. But again, all of us were at the mercy of COVID-19, and remote learning was used more than our schools would've liked.

For me, one of the most impressive aspects of life during the pandemic was the dedication of our county employees. Some of them worked around the clock, all of them put in crazy hours, more hours than they've ever worked before, and without complaint. I think about our heroic nursing home employees who cared for people they knew were infected with COVID. They went in and put on their PPE and helped our most vulnerable population. Our Broome County Transit drivers stepped up to make sure that we still had transportation. We had Office for Aging employees open our own county daycare at a senior citizen's center. All those centers were shut down, but we realized with schools closed, our essential employees would need daycare. We started out with three contact tracers from the health department. We now have seventy. And they are on the front lines day and night, doing what I consider the most important work we can do to prevent widespread infection.

COVID-19 has made a huge financial dent in our county revenues, all while we had to come up with the money to fight the virus. We had built up a large fund balance, which enabled us to counteract some of the shortfall. We have also enacted a strict hiring freeze, so right now we have hundreds of positions that aren't filled, and I have to offer more kudos to our employees who have covered some of the responsibilities of the unfilled positions. We were able to come up with a flat budget, but we are certainly hoping that the federal government and the state give us some financial aid.

We are at the beginning of the end of the pandemic. We've seen our infection rate go up, but we have redoubled our efforts to flatten the curve, and are better at managing the problems. It would be the height of understatement to say that it has been a tough ten months. No county executive, no matter how experienced, can rest easy knowing he or she has lost one resident to a flood or fire or blizzard or any natural disaster. By mid-January 2021, the virus had accounted for 228 deaths in Broome County, an unbelievable, heart-wrenching number, and while I know that I did everything I could for my county, I wish that I could have prevented the losses.

The vaccine has arrived, so I'm convinced that our best days as a community are right around the bend and, if we ever have to confront another crisis, we will be ready.

4

Chautauqua County Executive PJ Wendel

I call March 15, 2020, our day of infamy in Chautauqua County. That was the day I declared a state of emergency. By then, I'd served as the county executive for less than three months. And here is what I learned: there was no book on the shelf that said, "Dust this off in case of emergency."

Our first case was eight days later. A 103-year-old woman was admitted to the hospital for another issue. She had no symptoms of COVID-19, but she tested positive for the virus. She fully recovered and was discharged from the hospital. Tragically, others would not be so fortunate.

I put together a team to confront the problems I knew were on their way—the county public health director; three physicians; our emergency services director; the sheriff; and our logistical people. We worked on our approach to informing the public, making sure it was concise and easy to understand. We sent press releases to the newspapers and posted to Facebook, on my page and the page of the county health department. That evolved into a daily video as the infection rate rose—we were tracking the clusters by zip codes—and once the numbers started to come down, we appeared on fewer occasions until another uptick sent us back to our daily presentation.

One challenge we faced was that we're the only county in New York that borders Pennsylvania on two sides. Erie County is a dense population center, and Warren County is the opposite. Erie is a large shopping center, and Warren is home to a lot of commuters. Therefore, as Pennsylvania was opened, our economy shifted to another state; people were even dining out because Pennsylvania's restaurants were open before ours. So not only were we losing money that, with the pandemic and the shutdown, we couldn't afford to lose, but COVID-19 was being carried back and forth from shoppers and commuters, complicating our ability to track the spread.

There was a good deal of confusion as the executive orders came from Albany. People wanted the guidance immediately—because we've become a nation that has to have access to everything now—but it was often a couple of days before we could present it to our residents at our press conferences, explaining the orders and answering questions about them.

I relied on the sheriff and his deputies to deal with the PAUSE orders and complaints, and the sheriff spread them out to the jurisdictions they were in—whether it was the cities of Dunkirk and Jamestown or the villages of Fredonia, Falconer, and Lakewood—and made sure the right people could follow up.

During this period, the New York State Association of Counties helped enormously by rolling out a Take 5 for New York initiative, which encouraged residents to take the time to check in on their neighbors, an important part of passing along information and relieving the loneliness that for some—often the elderly—was a painful feature of the shutdowns.

And NYSAC's executive director, Stephen Acquario, had some excellent advice for us.

Steve said: "You need to act as if no one's going to help you. You're in this battle by yourself. You don't have reinforcements."

Steve wasn't being negative or critical, just underscoring that we needed to figure this out for ourselves, and we did that.

Our businesses were suffering; some were closed temporarily, and others were closed for good, and residents were losing their jobs. I knew our industrial development agency had $10,000 we could use for a loan program. It wasn't a significant amount of money, but to somebody who was going under it was life raft. We put out the information; the IDA started making loans; the businesses paid us back, and we made more loans.

While I was speaking to the IDA, I was told, "Hey, we have a guy from Jamestown Plastics, Jay Baker, who is creating a face shield."

I contacted Jay and went to meet him on a Sunday: I always wanted to be the guy in the field, seeing what our residents were doing. Jay said that he had a concept for a shield that could be attached to a visor or a hat. His son and a friend were working on it.

Sounded good to me. You can't have too much personal protective equipment.

By Tuesday, they had a prototype of the TrueHero face shield. The mold was polished so well that there weren't any creases in the plastic. It had ventilation ridges on top and the TrueHero logo on the bottom. So we put Jay Baker in touch with the mayor's office in New York City, and they were working to get the shields into the hands of healthcare workers in the city.

I was glad to assist a local business as it shifted to producing a new product that could save lives, and everybody I've talked to can't stop raving about the TrueHero shield.

That was only one example of how we tried to support our businesses who were shifting gears to fight the pandemic. One of the things that we are proud of in Chautauqua County is neighbors helping neighbors. Pace's Pizza, for example, was owned by a young man and his wife who had bought it and were ready to make a splash when COVID hit. I hated to see them get hurt by circumstances beyond their control. And the pizzeria put out a challenge to the community: buy a pizza and they'll match it. They were trying to sell a large number of pizzas in six or seven weeks. They reached their goal in a week, thanks to the Jamestown Police Department, Jamestown Fire, healthcare workers in long-term care facilities. All across the community people bought pizzas to keep the business afloat.

Our community also pulled together to feed children from impoverished families. Crown Street Roasters in downtown Jamestown and 5&2 Ministries were selling bag lunches for a dollar. People were donating to buy the lunches, and lunches sold out every day.

I've been thinking about a specific challenge we met that could be useful to the county leaders of the future. I'd have to say that was in late August of 2020, when the county faced two separate clusters of COVID-19 cases.

One involved employees at Fieldbrook Foods Inc.'s food manufacturing facility in Dunkirk. The other was among college students at the State University of New York at Fredonia. By September 22, there were eighty-nine individuals, either employees or close contacts of employees, who were associated with the outbreak at Fieldbrook; and 102 students at SUNY, who tested positive for COVID-19.

In both of these outbreaks, the Chautauqua County Health Department and my office, seeing the potential for a big uptick in cases, worked with officials from the New York State Department of Health to stop the spread of the virus. Our focus was on quarantining everyone who tested positive and their close contacts.

At Fieldbrook Foods, the county along with staff from the State Department of Health, our department of health and human services, emergency services, ALSTAR EMS, Fredonia Fire, and the Chautauqua Center conducted a testing event at the facility for all employees who wished to be tested. Of the 393 individuals tested, twenty-four were positive. Meantime, the county conducted a walk-through inspection with the State Department of Health and Ag and Markets to verify that the company was in compliance with prevention guidance. There were a few recommendations that were made about common areas, break times, and handwashing, which the company implemented.

We also worked with the Office for Aging Services and the sheriff to distribute food to individuals impacted by the Fieldbrook outbreak who had to isolate. Many of the people lacked family or community resources to assist them, and they needed baby formula, diapers, and cleaning supplies. We got together with the nonprofit and faith sectors to provide for their needs. Several COVID-19-positive individuals required alternative housing in order to isolate from their loved ones, and the county took care of them as well.

With the cluster at the college, the county health department and SUNY Fredonia issued a joint statement to students and faculty about the several scenarios they believed contributed to the spread of the virus on campus. In the statement, they called on individuals to limit assembling to less than ten minutes in common areas when face coverings are not continuously worn, have no visitors in the residence halls, and not attend large off-campus gatherings, which happened to be in violation of the state's order.

New York State deployed rapid testing machines to address various clusters in the Western New York region, and during one of our control room meetings I asked if some of the machines could stay with us to help contain future outbreaks, and the state let us keep four of them. In consultation with my team—both public and private partners—we created a rapid response plan. Now, if we have future clusters of COVID-19 cases, we can deploy these machines and setup a testing site where results are available in fifteen minutes. This would allow us to quickly identify and isolate positive cases and their close contacts and to mitigate the spread of the virus.

Today, in the middle of January 2021, we have 5,176 cases of COVID-19, and we've lost forty-six of our residents. The grief resonates throughout the county, and I have my own losses tugging at my heart: my great aunt and a cousin, both of whom resided outside of New York State, died from COVID-19 within a day of each other.

Yet we can look back with pride at our efforts. We lived up to the example of our grandparents' generation. We continued the tradition of what made America strong—doing our best to help our communities.

And we have hope. There is a vaccine now, the light at the end our tunnel. We have weathered the pandemic and, if we are ever unfortunate enough to be challenged by another pandemic, we will be ready to do all we can to protect our friends and families and neighbors.

5

Chemung County Executive Chris Moss

On March 4, 2020, our first organized meeting with the public health director, the sheriff, and six or seven people was held to review our emergency preparations in the event that COVID-19 ever came to our door. I wasn't worried. China and New York City are a long way from the Southern Tier. We do have the headquarters of Corning Inc. here, and the company had a plant in Wuhan, so we were concerned about their folks flying from Wuhan to our regional airport. It turned out that the Corning employees who visited China had been tested, and no cases were reported.

Twelve days later, in an act of caution, we closed the schools. Our first positive case of COVID didn't arrive until the end of March, and none of the 160 patients in our nursing homes were infected. By then, we were ready, with enough personal protective equipment. There was an uproar when the rumor spread that Governor Andrew Cuomo was going to take ventilators from our hospitals and move them to New York City, but fortunately that didn't happen.

By August, I thought that we had dodged a bullet. Then there was a cluster of positive cases from a church in the town of Horseheads. The infections were traced back to six other upstate counties. We had an additional cluster at Elmira College.

Across the county, COVID-19 was ballooning out of control. We closed the college. Our hospital beds began filling up. People were still attending church in these mass gatherings until the governor designated us an orange zone, limiting gatherings to ten people and closing down indoor dining in our restaurants.

People were upset by the closings. I was worried that we'd run out of hospital beds, especially in the intensive care units, and I was haunted by the televised images from New York City of those refrigerator trucks holding the dead.

I'd heard that there was a mass of COVID-positive cases in the two state prisons in our county—Elmira and Southport Correctional. As county executive, the prisons are separate from our operations, but now we got involved. It ended up being over five hundred inmates out of the 890 in Elmira prison. That was bad enough, but after people visiting the prisoners left, they went to stores and visited friends and family, and the potential for spreading the virus was enormous. I ended up calling the governor's office to say, "This isn't going to work. We need to know how the prisons will quarantine people."

Eventually, they closed down visitation, though I think the state could have done it sooner. We did so at the county jail, and we only had about a dozen cases there.

In the meantime, the county was suffering financially. With my long experience in government, I was accustomed to the ups and downs of budgets, but this was as bad as I'd ever seen. Our sales tax revenue was down; so was our revenue from hotels and motels and casinos. We made massive cuts, never easy given that so many of our expenditures are mandated by the state. We left over 120 positions vacant, canceled road projects, and took money from all forty departments in the 2020 budget. Our unemployment rate here is around 6.5 percent, which isn't too bad. There are jobs available, but until the federal stimulus money runs out or people think they're not going to get it anymore, you won't see people going back to work. Overall though, it seems like there will be no end to our financial pain. Certainly, there are businesses that won't survive or come back. The pandemic has so many tentacles. There are new challenges every day.

We received many complaints as understandably people were upset. The majority of them understood how tough a situation local government faced. We made sure to communicate the reasons for our decisions and to keep everyone informed. We held internal meetings five days a week. I've been with the county for over thirty years—sheriff for thirteen and the executive for the last two. In all of my time in government, I can count on one hand the number of times I'd spoken to the public health director. Now I was talking to Peter Buzzetti every day, and he was so good at his job that I felt the county was blessed to have him.

I also paid close attention to communicating with residents. A county executive is about as local a job as you can get—perhaps after the cop on the beat. And the key to doing the work well is talking to the people who need you. Mainly, I operated through Facebook, Twitter, and the county website, but we also held press conferences a couple times a week and held Q&A sessions at the end of those briefings that proved to be very popular.

I'm most proud of our communication with the community. My reward was that when I went grocery shopping or for a walk outside, people would come over and say, "You know what, I wouldn't want your job, and thank you for letting us know what's going on." As county executives, we are on the hook with residents. We're constantly out and about. We live in our counties; our spouses and children live there; and residents aren't shy nowadays. If you disappoint them, you will hear about it. This makes us more responsible. We know where the buck stops. No matter who might make a mistake in the county, it's our responsibility. And that, as far as I'm concerned, is how it should be.

One of our ongoing challenges was making sure the less fortunate among us had access to food. Thirteen (13) percent of our eighty-eight thousand residents live below the poverty line. We leaned on our meals on wheels and the Food Bank of the Southern Tier. We worked with them through co-sponsored events throughout the summer. To this day, we have sites at the Fairgrounds for people to come and get what they need.

A bright spot was the frequent contact I had with other county executives thanks to the New York State Association of Counties. I spoke to my counterparts once or twice a week. We're on a first-name basis, and we do what we can to help each other, and this wouldn't have happened without the pandemic. Democrat or Republican, it doesn't matter, not when the people who elected you are suffering.

At this point, in mid-February 2021, we've lost eighty-four of our residents to COVID-19, with 6,302 people testing positive. It is hard to wrap my head around the losses. I know we did everything possible to prevent them, but that doesn't make it any easier.

And we are struggling to get the vaccine. Everyone I talk to wants to be vaccinated, and they can't understand why we're only getting two hundred doses a week. In a county our size, it will take seven years to complete the vaccinations. That's how the state is doing things. It's so disorganized right now. I think there are too many cooks in the kitchen. The regional hubs don't know what the governor's office is doing versus the Department of Health. It's crazy. I know people are trying their best, but it isn't working for us. This week a half dozen of our residents drove to Plattsburgh to get their shot. That's four and a half hours from here. Seniors are making these trips, and they'll have to go again for their second shot in three weeks.

We have people signing up for the vaccine at three or four locations. Then they end up getting the vaccination and not informing us, so they remain on a list at other locations and take up spots that others could have used. Some people are scared that they'll never get the vaccine.

Had the state just given us the doses, I believe we could have distributed them much more efficiently. I had a plan. We had an old warplane museum that was empty, and we cleaned out the place and revamped it so we could vaccinate a thousand people a day. We called it a Mass Vaccination Center, previewed it to the media, and sent a letter to the governor, so I have a huge center sitting there with tables and chairs. We could have provided vaccinations to the entire county in three months if only we had enough doses.

My greatest wish is to protect my residents, and I only hope that I get the chance.

6

Erie County Executive Mark Poloncarz

Erie County sits along the shore of Lake Erie in the western part of the state, more than four hundred miles from New York City, so our first case of COVID-19 didn't arrive until early March. We had been keeping an eye on the virus as it traveled from New York City to Albany and finally to Buffalo. It gave us a couple of weeks to gauge our needs for personal protective equipment, and for our hospitals to plan for an influx of patients.

Its arrival was fast and furious. In those early months, we spent most of our time trying to acquire test kits and working with our nursing homes to protect patients and staff. We also consulted with the U.S. Army Corps of Engineers to plan for the conversion of our Buffalo/Niagara Convention Center into a COVID-19 field hospital. As it worked out, we didn't do the conversion, but the loading dock at the center would be used as part of a drive-through testing facility.

We were lucky that we knew what was coming because of the initial spread downstate. Yet, as in most other parts of the country, we were not as prepared as we would have liked. We didn't have enough PPE, and we relied on the CDC and New York State to get us test kits, though it took a long time for them to get here in the quantity needed. Since then, we have acquired millions of pieces of PPE and hundreds of thousands of test kits, so that we would be prepared for the potential onslaught in the fall and winter. I told my staff from now on we could never have enough PPE. If you thought that one hundred thousand masks and sixty thousand nitrile gloves would be sufficient, now we need two million masks and one million gloves. We will never be caught short again and we have sufficient supply to ensure we won't.

Today, those first months are as hazy as a bad, half-remembered dream. While most of Erie County was shut down and people were staying safe in their houses, we were coming to work and working twelve to fourteen hours a day. Our staff was working so hard it got to a point where I had to send people home because they were burning out—from the Department of Health, the Department of Homeland Security and Emergency Services, the Department of Public Works, and from my own office. I am proud of our team's efforts. Most of our citizens will never know how hard our county team worked to protect the public.

In the past, the county had gone through outbreaks—

hepatitis and tuberculosis—so we were experienced with point of care to treat our residents. We knew how to put together the bones of the program, but we never had to handle one as large as COVID-19.

Communication with our residents via press conferences and social media became crucial because it was the best way to let people know how dangerous this virus could be and what they needed to do to be safe.

On March 15, as COVID-19 spread through the county and I declared a state of emergency, we had to cancel our in-person press conferences and present them virtually. I would speak along with Dr. Gale Burstein, our commissioner of health, and Dan Neaverth from the Department of Homeland Security and Emergency Services. We'd talk about the latest facts and figures and what we were doing to address the situation, and then we would take questions over the phone. We did this every day for more than three months.

It was an effective way to inform the public, and I tried to do so in a calm manner to reassure the public of our actions and leadership. However, underneath my calm demeanor, I was worried that with a population exceeding nine hundred thousand, we'd run out of hospital beds, and thousands of residents would die. While we never did reach the death totals initially projected, as of February 8, 2021, 1,543 Erie County residents have died from COVID-19 and I do regret we could not save all of them.

Before COVID-19, our economy had been stronger than at any time during the last half-century. Unemployment was at a record low, and some tremendous new businesses had come to our region. The virus changed that, and one of the first things I did was to create a task force with business leaders and representatives from government and nonprofits to figure out how we could rescue our economy. It took a number of months, but I'm proud to say that we've dropped from nearly 20 percent unemployment, down to a little over 5 percent unemployment.

I think of working on the issues of economic distress as equivalent to helping parents find childcare or assisting families at risk of eviction or foreclosure: it was all part of the same response. You do everything you can and hope for the best.

I did find it necessary to let people know that obeying the rules on gatherings was important. We weren't afraid to go out there and write up a party if people were violating the law. Generally, we gave warnings if there was an incident at a bar or restaurant and it wasn't egregious. We would allow them to remediate it, and then come back to ensure things are in order. But if there were egregious violations, we handed out fines. It didn't take long for businesses to get the message, and since then they have generally followed the rules, and our community is safer and better off for it.

As the county executive, I understand that I'm in the spotlight and that residents hold me responsible for how we've responded to the virus. In my view, my staff and I and officials across the county have done a good job, and I'm proud of them. I was recently asked if I regretted any decisions I made during the pandemic. While I don't regret a specific decision because I've learned you can't change the past, I do regret that 1,543 of our friends and neighbors died from this virus.

I'm not one to make excuses, but as we have wrestled with the pandemic, I did wish that we had more latitude to make local decisions. I appreciate the things that Governor Andrew Cuomo has done to assist us, but there is a lot to be said for being able to respond immediately to a problem without having to get approval from the state. Those that are closest to the situation are in the best position to make decisions for the community. It is the basis of the command structure used to respond to emergencies, and it should be used in any future similar event.

In conclusion, after working very hard with our partners for almost a year, COVID-19 is still here and taking lives in our community. In fact, the highest total of new cases for any one day in Erie County was recorded not in the spring of 2020, but on January 6, 2021. More people died in December of 2020 than in any prior month.

It is tiring to constantly be responding to the pandemic, and it hasn't been easy, but that is what we must do to protect as many lives as possible. I have tried to keep an even demeanor throughout. I didn't want the public to think that we didn't know what we were doing. While there were times in which we were learning on the fly, we did know what we were doing—we were taking care of our residents using our training and experience.

7

Monroe County Executive Adam Bello

We had our first case of COVID-19 on March 11, a day I will never forget. Beginning in January, we had been following the pandemic as it creeped toward us, preparing for our first infection. We held regular media events, brought our hospital systems together, and offered what advice we could to the community, particularly about receiving flu vaccinations. We also met with United Way of Greater Rochester, designating them as the coordinating entity of the nonprofit community.

More cases quickly followed—two of them in our schools. At the time, we didn't understand how the virus was spreading, so we made a decision, in consultation with our school superintendents, to close the schools until we had a handle on what was happening. And just six days after our first case, we had our first death. The first of too many lives tragically lost, and particularly troubling because no one knew how the person had become infected.

Following our early cases, we declared a state of emergency to be able to take whatever actions were necessary to be able to slow the infection rate. For instance, when installment payments for property taxes were due, it was clear that we couldn't have thousands of residents, particularly older residents who might not have their taxes escrowed, showing up in clerks' offices to pay tax bills. We signed an executive order to prohibit the in-person paying of taxes, and then used the federal CARES Act dollars to waive processing fees allowing bills to be paid online. Knowing the financial disaster COVID-19 would cause, we also quickly started a small-business loan program. It offered zero interest with flexible repayment plans, and in the end, it helped to keep some businesses afloat.

As Easter, Passover, and Mother's Day approached, we knew that large indoor gatherings would be problematic. Rather than telling people that they couldn't get together—a dicey proposition at best—we talked to our community about how to gather in a safer way.

One of our earliest and most critical decisions in shaping our response to COVID-19 was that we would do it as a community. We convened our two hospital systems, local elected leaders, and the county health department to ensure we were collaborating and sharing the best, most accurate information available. Transparency was critical. Understandably, people were frightened, and it was our job to help to mitigate that fear, so we said: "The virus is here.

This is how it's being addressed. This is what we know, and this is what we don't know."

We kept that up with daily announcements on our case numbers and the clusters of infection, while also offering advice on how to respond. We used every platform. Our local media functioned as true partners in this effort. We provided updates on television, in newspapers, and on social media. At one of our briefings, I demonstrated how to make a homemade mask. Thinking back, it was a wild thing to do—interrupting *Days of Our Lives* so the county executive could do arts and crafts on live TV. But it worked. I spotted more than a few homemade masks during my next trip to the grocery store.

We also did a round of televised town hall meetings that included the public health commissioner, Dr. Michael Mendoza, Congressman Joseph Morelle, Mayor Lovely Warren of Rochester, and myself to answer questions about how people could address the pandemic in their own families or businesses or neighborhoods.

Every afternoon at two o'clock, I hosted a phone call with our local elected officials in the county to talk about what they were seeing, provide the most up-to-date information we had about what was going on, and to give them a chance to ask questions. And if I didn't have the answer, I'd find it and bring it back to them.

One major concern we had was how to keep supermarkets and other essential businesses open, while asking our community to stay safe at home. So we reached out to them to ask what they needed to stay safe. More often than not, the answer was personal protective equipment. PPE would prove to be a huge need, and we secured as much as we could, as quickly as we could, and provided it to our essential businesses for free.

This was something we continued to do as the pandemic wore on. When barbershops and hair salons finally reopened, everyone was waiting to get in. I think I had the longest hair I've ever had in my life. When the guidance was published, it said that barbers and hair stylists could reopen the next day, but they would be required to wear a face shield. I saw that and immediately asked, "Where in the world are they going to get a shield in the next four or five hours? I don't even know where to get one." It turned out that the county had them, so we offered face shields to every barbershop and salon owner in Monroe County. Over the next few days, we distributed thousands of them and did the same thing when restaurants opened to provide them with facemasks and hand sanitizer. We would eventually do the same thing again when schools reopened and provide millions of masks and other PPE to schools across the county.

PPE distribution was one of many ways we underscored our educational campaigns to take precautions. We provided masks to all residents of Rochester through the mail, and in the suburbs we did drive-through distributions. We were also able to partner with the city of Rochester and a number of community nonprofit partnerships to create the Six Feet Saves campaign, which included PSA commercials, lawn signs, and billboards educating residents about the importance of maintaining a physical distance. As spring approached and the weather got nicer, the campaign evolved to encourage people to go outside and enjoy the county parks, spray painting Six Feet Saves signs on the ground to give a visual detail of what the spacing looked like.

Early on, it was hard to see where the virus was spreading and if it was doing so disproportionately because we didn't have the ability to do community surveillance and mass testing yet. You could only test people who were symptomatic, and when there was a positive result that would change the course of their treatment. We knew there were a lot of sick people, but we didn't know who they were or where they lived. Once testing capacity expanded, we were able to see where clusters were developing, clearly showing that some of the harder hit communities were low-income populations and communities of color, particularly in certain sections of Rochester. Knowing that allowed us to respond. We concentrated testing there by working with community-based healthcare systems such as Trillium Health and Anthony Jordan Health Center to set up free testing in those neighborhoods and brought the sites to them.

Most important, we tried to give the communities strategies for being part of the solution. Instead of just scaring people into staying in their homes, we provided tools for how they could help out. Can you help an elderly next-door neighbor get food, so they don't have to go to the grocery store? Can we find new ways to celebrate holidays with our families while keeping our grandparents safe?

Can you pick up donations from the United Way? Because when people feel helpless, the best way to address their helplessness is to give them something to do.

* * *

It has now been ten months since our first positive case. We are in a new year, and the vaccine rollout is underway. Not long ago, we had shortages of PPE and were running out of morgue space. Now we have millions of pieces of PPE in storage and ready to go when needed. We fought hard and made sacrifices to flatten the curve. We went from not seeing our friends and families to seeing them once again, but outside, where we could be safe. And our schools are doing a phenomenal job keeping their students and teachers safe, while providing instruction in new ways.

Monroe County has lost 596 residents to the virus, each loss weighing painfully on my heart. We did a good job mitigating COVID-19 in the early months, but doing so spread a false sense of security across the county that, in its own way, was as dangerous as the virus. So we had to fight rising cases and rising hospital numbers again in the fall and winter. I will always wonder if I could have done more for the community when the virus surged. Hindsight, as they say, is 20/20. It also comes with waves of regret.

These days, when I get a rare quiet moment, I find myself thinking back to the weekend of our first fatality. I was stressed out about making the announcement, along with the other bad news—the cancellation of the St. Patrick's

Day parade and the closing of the schools. I mentioned to a friend that I was like the Bad News Bears, and he replied, "Adam, you're not the one who went out into the street and threw a vial of coronavirus on the ground to get everybody sick. You're the person who has to convey what's happening, and how the public is going to get through it."

For me, it was a good re-set moment, a moment of clarity. The job of a leader in the middle of a pandemic is to communicate and answer questions. You can't be afraid to give bad news or admit to not knowing the answers, all while reassuring people that you will do everything you can to figure it out.

I am proud of our community and how so many competing entities collaborated to solve the problems we faced. And I am grateful that I had a chance to do my share.

8

Montgomery County Executive Matthew Ossenfort

Dave Swart Sr. was a retired lieutenant and thirty-year veteran of the Amsterdam Fire Department. Dave spent his sixty-ninth birthday in the St Mary's Hospital ICU battling COVID-19, isolated from his wife of fifty years, Pam, and family. Keeping busy in his retirement and active in our community, Dave owned and operated a popular hot dog stand, Dave's Dawgs. His son, Dave Jr., had been my friend since we were kids.

I learned that Dave Sr. had become infected with COVID-19 from my public health director, Sara Boerenko, an Amsterdam native who knew the Swart family. When Sara called, I was in shock. As far as we knew, Dave Sr. contracted the virus out in the community. This was early, before wearing masks, social distancing, and frequent handwashing were widely practiced.

We are a small, predominantly rural county in upstate New York. The population hovers around fifty thousand. New York City is more than a three-hour ride from us. I was aware of the spread of the virus downstate, but I thought we might avoid that. When Dave Sr. was hospitalized, we only had twelve confirmed cases and no deaths. Pam helped to warn people by making Dave Sr.'s test results and hospitalization public. With visitation restrictions, the family was forced to gather outside the hospital, below his ICU room window. The fire department used the ladder truck to post a Maltese cross with written messages of encouragement from active and retired department members on the window. The community posted messages on the Dave's Dawgs food truck that he otherwise would have been preparing for the spring season. Updates on his health appeared in our newspapers. There was even an article that read, "Amsterdam man with COVID-19 takes a turn for the worse." The sub-headline was "We need a miracle. People gathered at St. Mary's to pray for Dave Swart."

On April 3, 2020, Dave Sr. passed away.

Restrictions prevented the family from holding a funeral, at least one in the fashion he deserved. Shortly after Dave's Sr.'s passing, he was brought home by his brothers of the Amsterdam Fire Department. The department honored him with a procession through Amsterdam which included a Last Alarm outside the department, passing by St. Mary's Hospital to honor everyone inside that helped in his battle, and concluded at Dave's home where his remains were presented to his wife and family. The procession was kept private to mitigate the spread of the virus, but many attended, staying in their vehicles, waiting for the procession to pass by the Church Street location of Dave's Dawgs.

The day of his funeral, there was a large procession from the fire department, the police, elected officials, friends, and family. People lined the streets to watch. I was in a car with Sara. Both of us were crying.

Following her husband's passing, Pam and her children Becky, Jen, and Dave Jr. became part of the Montgomery County family and now will forever be. Pam took to social media and referred to our Public Health Director Sara and the nurses as "Sara's Soldiers." We had shirts made with those words on them for the staff. In the beginning, our nurses would call homes to talk about dealing with the virus, and people would hang up thinking it was a prank or start screaming at them because they didn't believe the whole thing was real. The nurses experienced not only frustration but anger and, at times, verbal abuse. It was a constant back and forth from talking to a family member with a sick loved one to having somebody say, "Go scratch and stop bothering me."

The shirts reminded them that they were doing meaningful work.

A great reward of being a small-county executive is that you are in the trenches every day. I don't have a large staff, we do function effectively as a team, but I wind up being involved in much of what we do. I did the weekly and as needed COVID briefings along with Sara (and we posted on Facebook and Twitter as well). We concentrated on dispensing information, and I tried to persuade the community—even in the spring of 2020 when our infection rate was low—that we were not going to skate by the virus. There were rare moments of laughter. At one briefing, the sheriff and I were joking that we'd put on a few pounds and commented that the gyms were opening—not that either of us knew where they were.

Meanwhile, our emergency management director, Rick Sager, was busy on the phone trying to acquire personal protective equipment. He ended up getting a call from a woman named Retha Rochelle, who lived in Montgomery, Alabama. Sager said that he was listening to the voicemail from Rochelle with his wife, and his wife started crying. Rochelle and her sixteen-year-old-son William had been following the news about what was going on in New York State, and they wanted to do something to help. They are a family of faith, and Rochelle said her son has a heart of gold. Part of the message was from William, who said: "I wish I had more gloves to send, but this one box is all my mom and I could find. She had originally purchased the gloves for us, but when I saw a nurse on TV begging for help and I heard your governor say, 'Help us today and we will help you when it's your turn,' I wanted to do something to help. I wasn't sure you would want the one box, but my mom called the number we found online. We selected your county because of the similarities with Montgomery. I just wish I could do more."

They sent us the gloves, and when I heard the story from Sager, I attempted to inspire our county residents by telling the press that "We have been reminding everyone that we are stronger together. I guess this goes to show it doesn't matter which Montgomery County you live in. We are all able to unite as one and assist each other in a time of need."

It was great for getting some positive news out there, and it fit in with our campaign, "Stronger Together." And the story had a wonderful postscript.

One evening, months later, I was at home watching the news, and I saw an elected official from Montgomery, Alabama, talking about the situation there. The roles were reversed. They were in need of supplies, and we were fully stocked, and our cases were decreasing. I contacted Sara and Rick and told them it was our turn to help. We packed up a shipment, and I reached out to William's family and let them know we would be sending supplies. They were assisting their community through their church, and they were quite appreciative.

It had all come about because of one person's kindness. I still get a little emotional looking back on our connection to a family a thousand miles away.

* * *

We began considering the financial impact of the pandemic as we entered the lockdown. We understood how much of the state budget was reliant on New York City, and the city was inundated with cases and business shutdowns. Montgomery County had been through its ups and downs.

Once we had been a bustling industrial center until we suffered through a manufacturing decline, and since then we had been working to pick ourselves up. We are a resilient, gritty, blue-collar community, so I was confident that we would weather the challenges created by the pandemic. And so far, the county has been able to keep our finances stable. The impact on our local economy has not been as bad as some bigger communities. Our distribution centers, manufacturers, and big-box stores are all doing well. We are actually seeing some growth there. The mom-and-pop operations are taking it on the chin, and we're doing what we can to help. By and large, people are coping. They take walks, they use chalk to write messages on their driveway. We managed to ramp up our testing, and for a while we had the infection rate under control (which would change by January 2021 when new cases spiked).

However, I wouldn't say my biggest fear was financial. The emotional cost of the pandemic—the breakdown of mental health—concerned me the most. The impact of the lockdowns on Montgomery County, with its high poverty levels, is profound. In the more rural areas, we are social distanced by definition. On top of that isolation, there is insufficient access to services. In the "good years," I'd already dealt with these problems. For example, a family on the western end of the county with a child who is struggling with thoughts of suicide, trying to get forty miles down the road to access mental health services in Amsterdam. Say they don't have a car or a neighbor to drive them there, and then add COVID on top of that, it makes a bad situation worse. At one point, we had more suicides than deaths from the virus. Our domestic violence cases have been on the rise. So have incidents requiring the sheriff's office to respond. Add in the challenges of students not being in school, where that may be the one decent meal they get all day or the only situation where they can interact with a stable adult.

We're seeing drug overdoses, alcoholism, violence, theft, and vandalism. I lost my best friend to an overdose a while back, and we're doing our best to pull people and resources together. Yet when you're dealing with a rural community that does not have significant public transportation, a lot of issues go unnoticed. We're trying to combat all of this by joining the New York State Association of Counties Take 5 for New York program. If your neighbor is having issues, take a few minutes out of your day and get in touch via phone or social media and let them know help is available. It's a mutual aid undertaking. Not every problem is going to be solved by government. During the lockdown and the phased reopening, we did everything we could to encourage people to use the strength they had to assist those who were suffering through a weak moment.

Not long ago, we staged an event, Project Hope, to raise awareness about overdoses and suicide. So far, we've had eight suicides, which is higher than previous years. They all haunt me, but recently we had one in the Fonda-Fultonville School District that I suspect will stay with me for the rest of my days. We lost a young person I knew personally. She had given me a blanket when my wife was pregnant, and we used it in the hospital when my daughter had emergency surgery at four weeks old. And this sweet generous person, who battled serious issues, ended up taking her own life.

* * *

And so Montgomery County continues to fight COVID-19. By the first week of January 2021, we had lost sixty-one of our residents, and we had 1,602 known infections with more every day.

Our Public Health Department is making an all-out effort to keep up with the large volume of investigations. I am confident, particularly now that vaccines are available, that we will beat COVID-19. But our grief will last beyond the pandemic. And so will our pride in how we confronted this horrific virus.

9

Nassau County Executive Laura Curran

This chapter was previously published in The New Yorker magazine on November 16, 2020. It is reprinted with permission.

In late January, I was filling my bottle at the office water cooler when Lawrence Eisenstein, our county's health commissioner, sidled up to fill his own. Everyone in the office calls Lawrence "Dr. Larry." After medical school, he trained as an internist specializing in infectious diseases; afterward, he treated H.I.V. patients on Long Island. He became the county health commissioner in 2011. Three years later, when a man in New York City was diagnosed with Ebola, Dr. Larry made sure that our county, which is situated just east of Queens, had the right isolation and quarantine procedures in place. Even in normal times, he carries a tiny bottle of hand sanitizer in his jacket pocket.

"Doc," I said. "How worried should we be about this novel coronavirus in China?"

"I'll be honest with you," he said. "I've never heard my contacts at the C.D.C. sound so concerned, and they've been through SARS, MERS, H1N1." He paused. "That tells me they think it could have a significant global impact."

In my office, I started thinking about how we could prepare. Nassau County, where I was elected the county executive in 2017, is home to more than 1.3 million people. It covers four hundred and fifty square miles, stretching from the Gatsbyesque mansions on the north shore of Long Island to the middle-class neighborhoods of the south shore. Although it is mostly affluent, there are pockets of poverty and vulnerability. People who live in New York City often picture Nassau as a montage of beaches, porch swings, and shopping malls. My perspective is different: the government I run has a $3.3 billion budget and encompasses fifty-six independent school districts and a complex patchwork of cities, towns, villages, and hamlets. The county is more populous than Boston and Atlanta combined.

One way we plan for catastrophes is by running tabletop exercises: department heads and regional partners meet in a classroom-type setting to walk through what they'll do in case of a monster storm or a school shooting. I called Tatum Fox, my deputy for public safety, and asked her to organize such an exercise for the coronavirus. We settled on what we thought was an aggressive date: March 23. We didn't know that, by then, the time for exercises would have passed, and we'd be fighting the coronavirus for real.

Months later, during the summer, Nassau County would progress through the stages of its reopening. As the fall began, we would be diagnosing between twenty and forty new coronavirus cases per day, or about one case per forty-five thousand residents—a rate of viral spread low enough for us to start school and move toward a more complete reopening of our economy. Today, we think we are as prepared as possible for the growing winter surge; we're eyeing our numbers, which so far have ticked upward only modestly, with a full range of protocols and public-health options in place. But learning how to fight the virus hasn't been easy. Before the pandemic, our county government was focused on what we thought were big goals: revitalizing downtowns, fixing budget problems, building a new stadium for the Islanders. Suddenly, we were on conference calls planning the purchase of body bags and the leasing of refrigerator trucks as temporary morgues.

* * *

Along with other elected officials around the country, I found myself at the center of a kind of crisis I'd never experienced. In the beginning, it was like a dark storm, the sort you can hear even before you see the clouds roll in. Eventually, the clouds were all we could see. In such a crisis, every decision you make affects your constituents' lives and livelihoods. You do your best to balance it all: you talk to the experts, examine the numbers and the models, and seek the best advice. But the virus moved with overwhelming speed.

New York City became the worldwide center of the virus, and so it was bad in Nassau, too; our numbers were the highest outside of New York City. Since March, 52,897 Nassau County residents have tested positive for the virus, and 2,226 have died. In the early days, I'd catch myself thinking, Is this a dream?

Over the course of the spring and summer, Nassau managed to flatten its curve; we hope to keep it flat through the winter. But the virus is still circulating around the country, and, until scientists strike a definitive blow against it, with a vaccine or other treatments, all progress is provisional. Meanwhile, we are grappling with economic distress on an unprecedented scale. We need help for our businesses and citizens, many of whom have been thrown out of work. Our county government needs money for such basic public functions as safety, transportation, paving roads, and maintaining parks, but we also need money to continue fighting the virus: to fund more testing and contact tracing, and to maintain our ramped-up public-health infrastructure. We're building a dam, and the water is rising on the other side.

The coronavirus seemed to arrive in slow motion. In February, a month after our water-cooler conversation, Dr. Larry and the health department began monitoring two hundred and fifty people for signs of the virus. Most of them were travelers from China who had been identified by the Centers for Disease Control and Prevention, which was relaying news of incoming travelers to local governments. As soon as they landed, we contacted them, so that we could place them in quarantine and test them if they developed symptoms. At the time, our health department employed only six disease investigators, to respond to illnesses such as hepatitis and E. coli. The CDC hadn't yet given local labs approval to process coronavirus tests, and so we had to send our test kits to its lab in Atlanta. A hundred and sixty of the people we had contacted agreed to isolate themselves while we waited for the results. None of the tests came back positive.

On February 25, Dr. Larry came by my office, where I was meeting with my top aides, Helena Williams and Mike Santeramo, discussing the county's upcoming infrastructure projects. His expression told me that I should close the door.

"We may have a positive case," he said. A teacher had returned from a winter break trip to Italy and developed a fever and cough; she'd tested negative for the flu. She worked at Elmont Memorial High School, where, the following week, I was planning to give my state-of-the-county speech. A few days before that, I was supposed to meet with journalists at the school, for a "pre-speech on site." Without explaining why, I postponed it, in case the teacher's test came back positive and the school had to shut down. But it, too, came back negative.

It wasn't until March 5 that we got our first confirmed case, and its details couldn't have been more alarming. A forty-two-year-old man from Uniondale, who worked at a local hospital and had a side job driving people to the airport, came down with a fever and cough; his doctor decided to give him a COVID-19 test. Our health department's team of disease investigators got rolling. When was he last at work? How did he get there? Who lived with him? Had he been to any gatherings? Investigators discovered that he hadn't travelled. This was unnerving news: it meant that the coronavirus was already spreading in the community, circulating unchecked.

* * *

It's striking, after months of social distancing, to look back on my schedule then. Just a few days before, on March 2, I had traveled to Washington, D.C., to attend a of couple conventions; at one, the National Association of Counties, I sat with hundreds of other county officials in the ballroom of the Washington Hilton, while President Donald Trump briefed us on the coronavirus. (He spoke frankly and seemed to grasp that it was a serious issue. County governments would have an important role to play, he said, because they know so much about their residents.) My schedule on March 11 was similarly packed: after meeting with reporters from "Good Day New York," for a live sunrise segment about the coronavirus and visiting Northwell Health's labs in Lake Success to see their new virus-testing equipment, I stopped by the St. Patrick's Day luncheon hosted by the local Kiwanis club at the Garden City Hotel. When I walked through the double doors and into the ballroom, the event looked pretty much like it had every year. I wove through the tables, where everyone sat wearing green ties and sweaters; I said hello to the people I knew and introduced myself to those I didn't. Instead of shaking hands, I stuck out my elbow to bump—a wise move, I thought, given the viral threat. Still, I couldn't imagine the scale of what was coming. I didn't know that the luncheon would be my last non-coronavirus work commitment for months to come.

That afternoon, I met with Dr. Larry at a school administration building in Garden City for a conference with the superintendents of the county's school districts. Sitting at the head of a boomerang-shaped table, I scanned the superintendents' faces, which ranged in expression from worried to very worried. Since the first confirmed case, more had been found, including some in the schools. Two bus drivers had tested positive. Some districts, having discovered cases among teachers and staff, had closed individual schools; an entire district shut down for a week, after it found that all of its schools might have been exposed through a teacher with school-aged kids.

The Nassau County government doesn't control the schools—each district sets its own policies. Still, the superintendents seemed to be looking to me for guidance. I told them that I would support any decisions they made, including shutting down. "You know your schools and your communities better than anyone," I said. "But I am following the C.D.C. protocols for flu pandemic." I explained that, according to those protocols, closing schools is the last thing that a district should do in a flu-type pandemic: it's easier to contain the virus when kids are in class, instead of hanging out with friends or being watched by their grandparents. Many children rely on schools for lunch, and many healthcare workers and first responders depend on them for childcare. By this logic, closing schools was a step to take only when viral cases were skyrocketing.

In fact, we were already reaching that point. One morning, by the lockers at the gym, I took a phone call from Dr. Larry. He'd just been on a conference call with other regional health officials and learned that the New York City department of health was so hard-pressed that it was only testing patients who were hospitalized. That meant that, because the coronavirus is so often asymptomatic, most infected people in the city were going untested, and their contacts were going untraced. In Nassau, we were ramping up our test-and-trace operations. Dozens of staffers from our health department along with civilian members of the county police department were being quickly retrained as contact tracers—putting their regular duties, such as clerical work, on hold. But our border with Queens is more than fifteen miles long; many of our residents commute to the city. I could hear the frustration in Dr. Larry's voice. So many of the precautions we were taking wouldn't really matter; with the virus spreading unchecked next door, all the work we'd been doing could be quickly undone. (Since then, New York City's test-and-trace operation has expanded substantially.)

On Friday, March 13—two days after my meeting with the school superintendents—I learned that declaring a state of emergency would allow me to close the schools myself. I decided it was the best option. On Saturday I took my phone outside—I try not to be on the phone too much when I'm around my family—and sat on my porch swing, my jacket zipped up against the cold, and spoke with Dr. Larry, school leaders, and Governor Andrew Cuomo about how the school closures would work. I announced them the following day at a press conference. A few hours later at his own press conference, Governor Cuomo announced that he would be closing schools statewide.

That afternoon, knowing that it would soon shut down, I took my fourteen-year-old daughter, Julie, to the Roosevelt Field mall. Some stores had already closed; the mall seemed half empty. While Julie tried on jeans at American Eagle, I huddled in the corner, cupping the phone to my ear so that I could participate in a conference call with the governor, other county executives, and the press. I kept the phone on mute as much as I could, to block out the store's pop-music soundtrack. It was the last moment of routine. That day, we had twenty-three confirmed cases—within a week, we would have five hundred and forty-two. Two days later, on March 17th, a ninety-six-year-old man in Rockville Centre died of COVID-19—Nassau County's first confirmed death from the coronavirus. The next week, on March 20th, Governor Cuomo announced a shutdown for all of New York State.

We had entered a new stage of the crisis. The virus was out there, and its effects—and the effects of our efforts to contain it—would be felt in every part of society simultaneously. The clouds had rolled in.

Early in the pandemic, I'd organized regular conference calls with the five C.E.O.s who run Nassau County's eleven hospitals. On a call on March 27, the stress in their voices was clear. At the time, the press was focused on counting hospital beds. But, as one C.E.O. said, “Beds are easy.” The hospitals had turned conference rooms and residents’ dorms into spaces for new patients, and they’d built triage tents and negative-pressure rooms. On the grounds of SUNY Old Westbury, work had begun on a thousand-bed field hospital. What was a bigger problem was the strained supply of ventilators, staff, and personal protective equipment. On the call, three of the C.E.O.s said that they had enough ventilators to get through only the next few days. Others described rationing P.P.E. for nurses and doctors.

We began searching for ventilators and other supplies. Meanwhile, at meetings with my new business advisory council, we tried to come to grips with the devastating economic consequences of the state’s stay-in-place order. Rich Monti, who owns the Crest Hollow Country Club—a vast wedding-and-events space in Woodbury—told me, tearfully, that he’d sent his four hundred employees home meals made using all the food in the kitchens. Restaurants rushed to reconfigure themselves for takeout and delivery, while gyms, bowling alleys, and big-box stores simply shut down. Mom-and-pop shops, now stranded in ghostlike downtowns, laid people off. Within a few weeks, the number of residents applying for food stamps doubled.

Despite the fact that most people were staying home, crime was still an issue. Patrick Ryder, the county’s police commissioner, told me that his department was recording a ten per-cent increase in domestic violence calls; scams were on the rise, too, as grifters exploited isolation and fear. (One elderly woman called my office after receiving a phone call from someone purporting to work for her bank; the caller had said that her branch was closing because of the virus and asked for her Social Security number and banking information to "complete the transition" to a new branch.) We began coordinating responses to these problems. At the same time, our consumer-affairs office, which normally deals with professional licenses and matters of consumer protection, began investigating hundreds of reports of price gouging for products such as hand sanitizer and masks.

Urgent practical and bureaucratic challenges loomed simultaneously. At the county jail, our new sheriff, James Dzurenda—who'd been appointed by the legislature only on March 23rd—rushed to isolate infected inmates and secure adequate supplies of P.P.E.; each morning, he gave me an update on the number of infections at the jail. (At the time, just one inmate and three officers were infected; eventually, ninety-seven officers and sixty-five inmates would test positive.) I conferred with nursing home operators about their protocols. But we also needed to delay licensing and registration fees for home contractors and taxi drivers and to put off the collection of property taxes. We strategized about how to make sure the county could continue to provide everyday services: 40 percent of our revenue comes from sales tax, which cratered after businesses had shuttered. (In the month of April, our sales-tax receipts fell by thirty per cent.)

All the while, the virus did its work. People who'd been

infected before the shutdown were falling ill in increasing numbers. In February, I'd attended a Black History Month event in a community-center gym with Bishop David Gates, the African-American pastor of Miracle Christian Center in Hempstead; by March 26, I learned that he had died, at age fifty-six, from COVID-19. Not long afterward, the state began breaking down its mortality statistics by ethnicity. We saw that, although African Americans make up eleven per cent of Nassau's population, they accounted for 18 percent of our COVID-19 deaths. In general, poorer, nonwhite residents were getting sicker. In Hempstead, Freeport, Elmont, New Cassel, and other communities, the virus, which spreads more easily in tighter living quarters and multigenerational homes, was reinforcing long-standing health disparities. It victimized dense communities of color disproportionately.

As deaths mounted, burial became its own challenge. We established daily 4:45 P.M. calls between my staff and the crisis team at our Office of Emergency Management. The tone was professional, focused on the task at hand, but you could hear the concern in the timbre of the disembodied voices on the line. The news kept getting worse. In one call, I learned that the county's cemeteries were backed up, because of a work shortage; this, in turn, was causing congestion at funeral homes and hospital morgues. State guidelines advised against embalming bodies suspected of harboring the coronavirus, which meant that they needed to be refrigerated until they could be buried. We leased five refrigerated trucks and secured two refrigerated containers from the state; by building wood shelving, our public-works department increased each truck's capacity from eighteen to forty-eight. The last truck arrived on April 14. By that point, 1,001 county residents had died of COVID-19.

The virus seeped into all aspects of my life, into every waking hour. Running bought me some occasional escape. Before the pandemic, I'd been training for a half-marathon, either in the gym or at the high school track around the corner from my house. Now both were closed. Instead, I ran in the empty suburban streets. Discarded blue hospital gloves littered the corners. I put together new running playlists: alternative rock from the late eighties and early nineties, by turns angry, melancholy, sarcastic, boisterous, frustrated. I ran alone, outside, in the dark, listening to the Cure.

Every day at lunchtime, I held a press briefing on the coronavirus from the front steps of our county headquarters. Whatever the weather, I faced the cameras, usually with Dr. Larry and Patrick Ryder, the police commissioner. At first, we made the mistake of standing shoulder to shoulder; later, as the pandemic progressed, we switched to a distanced setup, standing six feet apart and speaking into separate microphones. I read out the numbers: positive cases, hospitalizations, patients on ventilators, first responders in quarantine, deaths. I applauded the tenacity, grit, and professionalism of our front-line medics, cops, corrections officers, deputy sheriffs, public-safety officers, volunteer firefighters, and E.M.T.s. I shared the guidance coming from the state and federal government. I tried not to scold or lecture. I wanted to let people know that what they were doing was working: they were adapting, staying home, flattening the curve, keeping our hospitals from being overrun.

All the same, it sometimes felt as though we ourselves were being overrun. On the morning of Sunday, March 29, I was sitting at my dining-room table, reading through the Sunday papers, when Dr. Larry called. Someone on his team had been diagnosed with the virus; Dr. Larry himself would now have to self-isolate, running the county's public health response from home.

Soon afterward, while I was giving my press briefing, a man driving by slowed his car and rolled down the window.

"Open the fucking county!" he yelled.

Adaptation, resourcefulness, a desperate, relentless, inventive scrambling for solutions—sometimes successful, sometimes not. Doctors and nurses began "splitting" ventilators, so that one device could handle two patients at a time. They used 3-D printers to make T-shaped adapters that allowed BIPAP machines, used for sleep apnea, to be repurposed as ventilators. They repurposed anesthesia machines. They rushed in nurses from other parts of their hospital networks and scavenged for staff from outside agencies. Our Office of Emergency Management ordered millions of masks, and we received P.P.E. from the state. We opened donation sites at Eisenhower Park and police headquarters. Businesses, foundations, faith groups, schools, and individual people dropped off boxes of masks, gloves, gowns, and sanitizer. Our public libraries used their

3-D printers to make face shields. On April 5, FEMA sent us ten ambulances, each staffed with two E.M.T.s. A couple of weeks later, they sent five more.

Food-stamp applications continued to skyrocket, tripling in April. We needed to get food to people. Evlyn Tsimis, the deputy county executive for economic development, told me that we should apply for half a million dollars in grants through a federal community-development program. I'm a Democrat, and the county legislature is Republican; still, we worked together to get the grants in a matter of days, funneling the money to food banks and Island Harvest, a nonprofit. I visited a food-distribution site in Roosevelt—one of fifteen in Nassau County. I'll never forget how hundreds of masked people, holding empty bags, waited quietly in a line that snaked for block after block.

Dr. Larry continued to run our health response out of his house in Bellmore. From there, he supervised a growing staff: by early April, we'd retrained hundreds of people from across the county government and police department to work as contact tracers, with roughly fifty operating at any given time. We enlisted others to staff a twenty-four-hour COVID-19 hotline. We also checked in on those who were isolated or quarantined—calling them, dropping by their houses, asking them to wave from a window. People who had worked the same job for twenty-five years were now collecting grocery lists and dropping off shopping bags at the homes of those quarantining. We took our workers out of their comfort zones; almost no one complained.

Early in the pandemic, we'd sometimes given mixed

signals: wear a mask; no, save them for first responders; actually, wear them, please! Now we did our best to cut through the confusion and speak to the most vulnerable. We invited faith leaders from poor neighborhoods to talk at our press conferences and made sure they wore masks. We worked with Federally Qualified Health Centers—public or private clinics situated in areas with a high percentage of Medicaid patients—to set up parking-lot testing tents. We knew that our testing and tracing efforts would only be effective if they reached the people—essential workers, immigrants, the poor—who were at the highest risk of catching the virus.

In the second week of April, I was sitting across from my aide Helena Williams at the round table in her office, where we had gathered for our daily 4:45 P.M. call with Emergency Management, trying not to munch through her whole bowl of Werther's Original hard candy; John Chiara, who runs compliance and procurement for the county, sat cross-legged in his usual spot in the opposite corner of the room. "The number of people going home from the hospital today is larger than the number of new patients being admitted," Dr. Larry told us from his house. "If that trend continues, that means we are entering the plateau." It took me a moment to process what he was saying.

As the news sunk in, I felt a loosening of tension in my chest—tension that had been intensifying all these weeks, like a rollercoaster slowly going up, up, up. The numbers held: two days, then three days, then two weeks in which the healthy outnumbered the sick.

Before the pandemic, we had been focused on revitalizing the county's downtowns. Young people who'd grown up in Nassau were fleeing the suburbs where their parents had settled because they were too expensive and not enough fun; New Jersey—New Jersey!—was developing the affordable, walkable neighborhoods that they wanted. Some of Nassau's mayors had been approving construction of new apartments within walking distance of Long Island Rail Road stations. Ralph Ekstrand, the mayor of Farmingdale, had followed this plan to great success: the new apartments there had filled up, and Farmingdale's Main Street, once desolate and soulless, had become a bustling hub of restaurants, bars, and shops. "Right now, it's a ghost town," he told me, over the phone. From my office in Mineola, I looked out my window onto the quiet street below. "Downtowns in Nassau County are dying," he said.

I heard the same from other mayors and from chambers of commerce and small businesses all over the county. Walmart and Target were thriving: they sold food and were deemed essential. But many independent shops couldn't make payroll or rent. After my conversation with Ekstrand, I walked out into the early-afternoon sunshine and at my daily briefing announced the twenty-second straight day of declining COVID-19 hospitalizations. The first wave was receding. Could we venture onto the beach?

The numbers were, in fact, beginning to suggest that we could reopen slowly but safely. They indicated that, after months of social distancing and isolation, viral circulation had dropped to relatively low levels. At the peak of the wave, half the people we tested had been positive; by mid-May, only ten per cent of tests were generating positive results. We were now finding that the vast majority of hospitalized patients—eighty-three per cent—had been isolating at home when they got the virus; our antibody tests, meanwhile, showed that just around twelve per cent of front-line workers had caught it.

All these signs pointed to the fact that, with proper P.P.E. and social distancing, we could return to work without taking on a substantially higher level of risk. At that point, Long Island had met five of the seven goals laid out by Governor Cuomo for phased, regional reopening. "There will always be risk," I said, at one of my Saturday briefings. "But we can minimize that risk. We can protect the vulnerable and get life cranking up again."

As a county executive, reopening isn't in my control. Governor Cuomo's executive orders and timelines supersede anything I can do locally. Based on conversations with him and his team, I knew that he was concerned about a new spike in infections. Dr. Larry agreed, and I got it—I really did. But I also knew that the longer we delayed reopening the harder it would be for many businesses and households to recover. As the owner of a commercial real-estate firm said, on one of my Zoom calls, "The price of perfection is bankruptcy."

I began visiting businesses, gyms, shops, restaurants, bowling alleys, pools, beaches, movie theaters, and hotels, talking with proprietors about their reopening protocols; I saw firsthand the sanitizing, social-distancing, and air-filtration measures they were putting in place. Months into the pandemic, with less than thirty new cases each day, we had a pretty clear idea of what kinds of activities spread the virus.

Practically no one was catching it while shopping in a store where everyone was masked; on the other hand, nearly a quarter of the new cases were traced to people who'd travelled to states with big outbreaks. Often, we found the newly infected when they got sick and saw a doctor, or through on-the-job testing. Many skewed young. They should have quarantined on their own; instead, we quarantined them. Our tracing corps had become a well-oiled machine: when a teenager who'd gone to three parties in three days tested positive, we found all of her hundred contacts, moving steadily from friend to friend. We benefited significantly from the fact that, in the summer, Nassau County residents spent lots of time outside; the virus is less likely to spread in the back yard, and even less likely on the beach.

This fall, most school districts in Nassau County were able to reopen. But we've been testing everywhere and watching the data: in the town of Lawrence, schools closed after an uptick in positive tests turned its district into what the state calls an "orange zone." Other districts have closed for a day or two after an increase in their case-positivity rate. In November, we began to see an increase in positive tests more generally. We're nowhere near the levels we experienced in the spring, but we're watching. "We're not out of the woods yet," Dr. Larry told me recently. He now carries two bottles of hand sanitizer with him—the second just in case.

Around the country, the response to the pandemic has often been hyper-politicized. Looking back on our experience with the coronavirus so far, I see missed opportunities and lessons learned, but I am proud of what we did right, what we figured out, and how we were able to do it together. Not everyone in Nassau County agrees with one another. We have the full spectrum of opinions here, from anti-maskers who want to “open the fucking county” to people who e-mail me every day to report mask violations. But there is a shared appreciation for common sense and an understanding that we are reliant on one another’s health and success.

Counties, not states, are the governmental entities on the front lines of the pandemic. In Nassau, the county runs the local health department with its communicable disease investigators and emergency responders; it coordinates with hospitals and distributes P.P.E.; it manages social services, public safety, infrastructure, and outreach agencies; and it works with schools and businesses. Nassau County is currently projecting a $750 million deficit for this year and next. I am lobbying hard for aid from the federal government, but with the dysfunction in Washington, it is seeming less and less likely to arrive. In the meantime, we are refinancing our debt at extraordinarily low interest rates, using the more-than-hundred-million-dollar surplus we accumulated last year, and continuing tight fiscal discipline, so that we can keep the county running with services intact. Our workers are out there, paving the roads. Many counties around the country will be in worse shape. Local governments need help.

In late January, we rushed at breakneck speed to respond to the coronavirus, improvising and scrambling. Today, we're in a different position. Schools, businesses, and households have adjusted. Our testing infrastructure is nimble; our hospitals are experienced; members of our just-add-water army of contract tracers have returned to their regular roles but can come back at a moment's notice, making calls, waving at windows. We think that, maybe, we've learned how to do this. Our hope is that we've learned enough.

10

Oneida County Executive Anthony Picente

In early March, as the world was learning more of what was to become a pandemic, a situation occurred in my community that proved to be the precursor of what was ahead. Two local physicians, a husband and wife, returned from Italy with symptoms of COVID-19. They began seeing patients before they felt too sick to go to work and canceled the rest of their appointments. That incident set off a rush of panic in the community, and it then became evident that we were dealing with something different than a run-of-the-mill illness. Both physicians tested negative for the virus, but people were becoming noticeably anxious.

On March 13, 2020, I declared a state of emergency across the county and closed the schools. We had yet to have a positive case, but the virus was spreading, and I knew it was only a matter of time. The next day, a Saturday, my staff along with other essential department heads went to the office. Our health director and I met with the director and chief physician of our regional medical group to discuss testing capacity, and to get their perspective on what we would be facing. After hearing their predictions, I couldn't sleep that night. I resolved that on Sunday we would take more actions and engage the entire healthcare network and all of our resources in a comprehensive plan. I've often said there is no playbook in times of crisis. In this case, that was never more true. But of one thing I was sure: we had to act fast.

I was just beginning my fourteenth year as county executive and had been through a variety of emergencies. I know that in any emergency, communication is essential on a variety of fronts. First, letting people know when and how they could get their information. Second, making sure it was clear and concise for all to understand. Third, letting them know that those in charge know what they're doing.

We began daily briefings on that Sunday, and the briefings would continue for months. We told the community our current case numbers and the helplines they could use to get questions answered and to connect with frontline workers. I spoke to my counterparts throughout the state sharing ideas and actions on how we were dealing with the pandemic.

As in other emergencies—and, in my opinion, even more crucial in this one—reacting calmly made people feel secure. When storms and flooding occur, they generally affect a specific town or neighborhood, and the response can be more direct in those areas. This virus would affect everyone and often in unusual ways, and so speaking with optimism and confidence was critical to tamping down the understandable fear that was loose in the county.

In those early days, we were challenged by the fact that we'd yet to have a positive case, and people needed to understand why we were taking such aggressive actions. I realized that while everyone was hearing from the president and the governor, they also needed to hear about the local situation. As the days went on, and I was holding daily briefings, I was overwhelmed by the response and understood more than ever the impact we were making. At a time when the world was in crisis, the community wanted to hear what was being done from the leader of their county. It was a position I'd been in before, but this was different, and I felt it. The magnitude of the virus reverberated in every sentence, every number explained, and it was exhausting. What was most difficult was watching the numbers grow and getting the sheets each day with the list of positive cases. One of the most trying days was announcing the first death and knowing that there would be more. Again, a major difference in this emergency.

A defining moment of our fight against COVID-19 was when we put the first mandatory public mask order in place more than a week before the state took such action. It showed our residents that we'd take any action, even the most controversial (at the time) to curb this virus. Leadership requires bold action, and I was not afraid to use what was at my disposal to keep people safe.

During it all, I was inundated with calls and emails

from people thanking me for the information and the words of comfort. There were those who were angry about venue closures and restrictions, but for the most part, people welcomed the daily updates. Unquestionably, the letters that hurt the most were from those who couldn't see their loved ones in nursing homes. My parents were deceased, but my wife's folks are still with us, and I couldn't fathom not being able to visit them, and the virus spreading in those facilities like wildfire. It is still painful as it continues today. I will never get over that feeling.

I'm still greatly concerned for our healthcare workers in the hospitals and nursing homes. They have been working tirelessly from the start, putting not only themselves at risk, but also their families. The major concern in every area was—and continues to be—whether a major outbreak would create a loss of those workers essential to care for not only COVID patients, but for all of our patients regardless of their ailments.

Our county government never closed, and even when executive orders required a reduction of in-house staffing, the vast majority of our workforce was on the job. The staff of the health department has been working seven days a week doing contact tracing. We also cross-trained many employees, who due to the various shutdowns of the courts and other areas, were available to assist in this process.

I am immensely proud of our entire staff who came up with so many different ways to keep people informed and engaged, as well as providing activities for children during the lockdown. From indoor activity drills to outdoor art contests, the creativity and concern were overwhelming, and came from so many valued employees.

Throughout this time, county government still had to function. The pandemic, while closing down various government centers, could not close the one that provides the most direct assistance to residents. The challenges of keeping it running while a great deal of the community was on PAUSE, and while spending was increasing due to personal protective equipment and overtime, was overwhelming. All coupled with the severe reduction in revenue made for difficult decisions. The choices, while painful, were simple. We needed to cut areas and programs that were not immediately essential or could not be completed due to the pandemic, and we had to withhold payments to other governments and agencies. There was no other way that the county could provide for our first responders and our residents without making these choices. I reached out to all leaders of other governments, from cities, towns, and villages, to explain our situation. We all had to share the pain. The greatest concern was just how bad the pandemic would get and whether our reserves could meet the rising tide. So far, so good. Yet we face an even greater challenge in 2021 until the vaccines end this scourge.

There are so many stories to point to throughout this crisis. Some of the most touching moments came from those patients who endured weeks in the hospital and were given a parade by their caregivers as they went home, and the drive-by parades of family and friends. In speaking to some survivors, as they like to be called, the connections they felt to their caregivers could not be more emotional. Since family members were not allowed visitation, nurses, aides, and physicians became their family. The bonds created, they say, will last a lifetime—a lifetime that was certainly extended by those caregivers.

As of this writing, we continue each day tracking the virus and working diligently to stop the spread. Our county workforce stands at seventeen hundred employees. We have had less than twenty cases in our workforce. I happen to be one of them, though I'm asymptomatic, and it is a testament to the vigilance by all of our employees, who, while continuing to serve the public, have demonstrated how to prevent the virus from spreading wildly throughout the workplace. We continue to work with employers across the county to help them navigate the state's guidance and to use best practices to keep people safe. We have assisted our school districts reopening and have established a direct line for them with our health department to deal with issues in real time.

All of these and so many more government actions have held our infection rate at the lowest of levels. It is what county government does every day. We have responded in hundreds of emergencies over the years and have reacted tremendously in this crisis. As I mentioned, we were given no playbook by the state or federal governments to deal with this. And that's fine because when all is said and done, county government will have written its own playbook, as we have done time and time again.

11

Onondaga County Executive Ryan McMahon

Located nearly 250 miles from the epicenter of COVID-19 in New York State, Onondaga County had the benefit of understanding how COVID-19 affected our neighbors in the Hudson Valley and New York City before the virus reached our community. The devastation would be undeniable, and we moved quickly to activate our plan to mitigate loss and keep people safe.

Our first confirmed case of COVID-19 occurred on March 16, but our teams in Emergency Management and the Health Department had been preparing for months. With a state of emergency already declared and an aggressive campaign underway encouraging people to practice physical distancing, we quickly moved to bring together all of our community partners, including hospitals, local governments, epidemiologists, and others to ensure we could take decisive action as the data warranted.

We partnered with a local health center and set up community testing. Just as important, we made efforts to ensure that our neighbors who lived in communities often hardest hit by public health emergencies had easy access to the resources they needed to stay safe.

Schools were shut down, but not before ensuring every district had a plan to take care of their most vulnerable. We know that for many children, school is the only place they receive at least two meals a day, and we worked tirelessly to make sure that those children continued to be fed. We also partnered with Childcare Solutions to arrange for our first responders, essential employees, doctors, nurses, and nursing home staff to have childcare. If these folks could not get to work during the pandemic, then the entire system would collapse.

Acquiring personal protective equipment was—let's say—challenging. The PPE chain was the Wild, Wild West. Masks that you could get for under a dollar were now eight or nine dollars. People reached out to us who miraculously had contacts in Singapore, China, and Taiwan for a small advance of $500,000. Legitimate governments, however, do not make these deals. We pressed on, qualifying different supply chains, and finally bought PPE at decent prices. We even secured ventilators in the event that we needed to transform the Manley Field House at Syracuse University into a hospital.

At the heart of our response to COVID-19 was our

communication with the public. We held briefings twice a day, once via Facebook Live at noon and another briefing with the press at three. These briefings were televised across Northern and Central New York and we took the opportunity to emphasize that we are all in this together and it would take everyone doing their part to ensure our community emerges stronger than before. As New York State continued to shut things down and we asked people to modify their social behavior, I was heartened at the number of people listening and buying in to these sacrifices they were being asked to make, as scary as they were. We spoke about testing, quarantines, the number of cases, food security, daycare, and mental health programs—everything that was relevant to the well-being of the public. Our job was to tell the truth without the slant of politics. We were asking people to sacrifice, and they had to know why. I never Monday-morning quarterbacked the decisions at the federal or state levels. I just talked about how they impacted us, and I believe people appreciated our straightforward approach.

Emotionally, the loss of life was overwhelming, but I knew the unintended consequences of these shutdowns would be severe. Whether it was individuals unable to identify or report domestic violence or child abuse to the rising cases in opioid overdoses or just the sheer devastation of our local economy, the human toll of this virus extended beyond what anyone could have imagined.

We were shut down for months and lost millions of dollars in sales tax and our room-occupancy tax essentially evaporated. We had to cut county government and execute rigorous austerity measures. Twice we offered retirement incentives, but still had to implement furloughs, voluntary and involuntary. We were facing a $70 million to $80 million shortfall as we prepared our next budget. Adding salt to the wound, our population is 461,000, just shy of the half a million federal requirement to receive at least $100 million of CARES Act funding.

So there we were, in the middle of a pandemic, with no money, letting go of staff and enforcing a host of new rules and policies including enforcing mask wearing and physical distancing, necessary to keep our community safe. No upside to this, really, except that when businesses were finally able to reopen, they understood what was at stake. We did institute a system for residents to send concerns or complaints about establishments not following safety guidelines and we teamed up our legal, probation, and health departments to investigate them.

State agencies would eventually also lean on us about complaints they received, asking us to investigate. More often than not, we learned our business owners simply did not understand or know all of the new rules they were being required to follow, and after empowering them with the necessary information, they quickly and gladly complied. At the end of the day, I am proud to say that our local restaurant industry willingly agreed to be our partners when it came to enforcing the rules. Neither we nor the restaurant owners had any interest in seeing them closed again, and we worked together to make sure that didn't happen.

As difficult as these last ten months have been, as a county we have many things of which to be proud. On top of the list is how the community came together, everyone pulling in the same direction. We planned and prepared for the needs of our residents, and we acted. There was no paralysis. Whatever the obstacle, we figured out a way to get it done. We were especially aggressive about testing—symptomatic and asymptomatic—which is one reason why we saw our positive infection rates drop as we began our restart. We were intent on finding those hidden asymptomatic cases because we saw what the virus was doing to our seniors. Therefore, we tested in assisted living facilities and independent living facilities to box in the virus.

We were equally aggressive in our schools. We deployed county personnel to perform asymptomatic testing and saliva-pool testing for teachers. Simultaneously, we were building up the infrastructure every day so that we could quickly pivot once the vaccine arrived. Syracuse University was also planning on using the Upstate Saliva Test to bring their students back, an effort which would provide a desperately needed boost to our local economy. However, it had yet to get emergency approval from the state or the FDA. Two weeks before school started, they had a decision to make. We were telling them they needed to test the students before they came back, and we knew it was a big ask because it was going to cost them $2 million. Syracuse University proved once again their commitment to our community and spent the money doing the right thing for public health. Testing kits were mailed to the student's homes, they self-administered the test, returned them, and were sent the results. Our community then knew which students were positive before they returned and required them to stay home and isolate. Those with a negative test were allowed to return, but our efforts did not end there. When the kids got to campus, they were tested again and thanks to this impressive undertaking, Syracuse had a great start to the school year.

We were also able to give some relief to small businesses, especially our hard-hit restaurants which are an important source of pleasure for our residents and tax money for the county. The Industrial Development Agency appropriated $500,000 to cover the cost of COVID-related expenses—tents, heaters, fire pits, and more, so that outdoor dining could be more comfortable and compensate for the loss of capacity indoors.

Our community spent months planning, preparing and mitigating; now we are waiting to for the vaccine. While nothing has made me sadder than the hundreds of people we have lost to COVID-19, nothing will make me happier than to start dispensing the vaccine so we can begin to reclaim our lives and move forward, together.

12

Ontario County Chairman Jack Marren

This book was commissioned by the New York State County Executives' Association, which is an affiliate of the New York State Association of Counties (NYSAC) and includes the counties that have an elected county executive as the head of their government. I am not a county executive. But I am the president of NYSAC, the chairman of the Ontario County Board of Supervisors, and the supervisor of the town of Victor. This chapter is dedicated to the county leaders—the board chairs, administrators, and managers—who stepped up to serve their communities and protect their residents during this pandemic. Their individual stories may not be in this book, but we honor and appreciate their collective heroism.

* * *

I had open heart surgery on November 12, 2019 and didn't return to the office until the first full week of January. We were watching what COVID-19 was doing in New York City, three hundred miles away, and thinking that it wasn't an imminent threat to us. I had a meeting with our public health director a few days before infections really spiked in the city, and we didn't talk much about COVID. Looking back, that was a missed opportunity, but we weren't anticipating an explosion.

As we monitored the situation downstate, there was a slow realization that the virus was headed in our direction. This was the first time in eight years as the incident commander for the town and county that I'd declared a state of emergency. We'd had a number of snow emergencies in which the sheriff put out travel advisories, but nothing like this.

I met with our school superintendents which we laugh about now, because our meeting was an old-fashioned conference call. No Zoom or WebEx had been introduced at that point. The time frame of a state of emergency spans about thirty days and we spoke about the timing of our plans, messages the superintendents needed to get out to their communities, and the importance of not igniting panic.

COVID-19 arrived here about the third week of April as a result of a husband and wife who had been at a conference in Florida. Our geographic location concerned me because we border Monroe County, a much larger area including the city of Rochester, where many Ontario County residents commute for work. I knew we were at an increased risk based on that fact.

I realized that we needed to put together an emergency management team and get a handle on equipment needs. I pulled leaders from the ambulance corps, fire department, and code enforcement. I was impressed with how structured and disciplined these individuals were. They were an outstanding resource for keeping departments across the county safe. Representatives from these groups made up a good portion of our town COVID-19 Committee.

The speed of events was disconcerting, and as the infection rate rose, residents began to worry. I knew next to nothing about COVID-19, particularly the risk to me with my health issues, and my family was increasingly concerned about my working at the office. When the pandemic hit, I was going to cardiac rehab at the Thompson Hospital in Canandaigua three days a week. They shut that down, which was a huge adjustment mentally because I wanted to do the right thing for my health, and I was scared. I'm still scared.

On Easter Sunday, I got a nosebleed. I was on two blood thinners and couldn't get the bleeding under control. We called our neighbor, a nurse, who said, "Jack, go to the emergency room." With COVID-19 patients showing up at the ER, that was the last place I wanted to be, but I was still bleeding heavily and had no choice. My wife dropped me off as she wasn't allowed to accompany me. I went in with a towel on my face. This provided me with the horrible experience of all the patients infected with the virus, or just in need of treatment, who are forced to face their treatment alone. It made me think about the families who are forced to wait for a phone call telling them the outcome of a loved one's operation instead of being by their side. That breaks my heart because I know how important my family was to me after my heart surgery.

When the nurse saw me, she said, "Sir, you need to have a mask on," and I pulled the towel away to show all the blood. They stopped the bleeding, and I had to go back three days later to have my nose cauterized, and I got a close look at the efforts hospitals were taking to keep patients and medical personnel safe. The doctor who attended to me was dressed like an astronaut and sweating profusely. I realized—here I am, a government official juggling my responsibilities, but the doctor was struggling to do his job as well while day in and day out confronting an increased possibility of infection. At my briefings, I always praised our healthcare professionals, and whatever praise I'd offered, it wasn't enough.

* * *

I'm a conservative, as is our county overall. When Governor Andrew Cuomo put us on "PAUSE" and businesses were being shut down and hurting, we received phone calls complaining about it. People were annoyed, but not overly aggressive. The mood changed when the governor announced that he was going to send the National Guard through the state to retrieve ventilators because he needed them in New York City. I'd spoken to the leadership of our hospitals in Ontario County and was informed that they had shared resources with New York City but were holding onto some ventilators in case we had a serious spike. I received multiple phone calls from residents, certainly many of my hunting residents and owners of multiple firearms, who declared, in the strongest possible terms, that I couldn't let this happen. In our region, it's often said that the Second Amendment is written in the heart of individuals. I laughed when one individual said, "Jack, I keep a damn copy of that amendment right next to my phone." Less amusing was when I heard from others that they intended to line up around the hospitals with their weapons to make sure the governor didn't try to take either our ventilators or their firearms.

The county was adamant that we were going to hold onto our equipment. Thankfully common sense prevailed, and the state went in a different direction.

In the meantime, I delivered a dark economic picture to the town of Victor and the county Board of Supervisors. Ontario County is fortunate to have a regional mall that averages $1.1 million a day in sales. With the mall shuttered, we weren't getting that income, and we'd never recoup it, so I projected that we could lose upwards of 50 percent of our sales tax revenue.

We made the necessary cuts, exploring various out-of-the-box programs, all while holding out hope—like many local governments—that the state would offer a retirement incentive. They did not. So we came up with one at the county, and saved a few million dollars, and we pushed off some capital projects.

We continued educating the public and communicating through our state and regional COVID-19 phone calls.

Half the time I wasn't sure whether it was Monday or Thursday because we were working nonstop, taking phone calls from residents, managing internal communications, and organizing phone calls with school superintendents.

From day one, our New York State federal delegation has supported us, and I can't thank them enough. Congressman Tom Reed, a true champion of local government, has been a silver lining for Ontario County and the entire region. He never failed to take my phone calls and answer questions, and he fought for us to get additional equipment and stimulus money.

* * *

Before working full-time in government, I was in operations for a large wine and liquor distributor. That background has really helped me through the pandemic because, in wine and liquor operations, you do 40 percent of your annual business from October to December, and it is crucial that you have all of your resources—manpower, forklifts, trucks, boxes, and the product itself—on hand, and that you adhere to a strict schedule.

This was excellent preparation for lining up and working with the emergency management folks, fire departments, schools, whatever else was needed to manage the pandemic. We're fortunate that our core group of key department heads—county attorney, human resources, finance, and information technology—have always been first-rate. We worked together, via Zoom, in the same way as COVID-19 committee, but with social services and the sheriff. Our major focus was determining what was essential for our COVID-19 budget, and how we could safely bring back our workforce. The first order of business in our meetings was to receive an update from the health department, detailing our positive cases, hospitalizations, the number of patients in the ICU, and those under the fourteen-day quarantine.

Many of our employees were working from home, and we sent them updates and checked in to make sure they were OK. We were all anxious about their families' health and the health of our employees. For those coming into work, we were quite militant about their wearing masks and social distancing. I recall having to have—let's call it a chat—with some highway superintendents who needed to reinforce these policies. They were wearing masks, but sitting side by side. I said, "This makes no sense because if we have one positive case, now I'll have to quarantine the entire group. If there are seven of you in the break room, those seven go on quarantine, and what happens when we have a snowstorm? I'll have no one to plow the roads."

When I put it to them that way, they did much better. A few times, I saw town trucks going by with two individuals in the truck not wearing a mask. So again I had to pick up the phone and make the point that this is serious and the rules aren't to be ignored. It was constant educating and re-educating. In the fall, we had an uptick in the region, and we had to step up our efforts with the town, the county, the schools, and the residents.

By the middle of January 2021, we'd lost seventy-five

Ontario County residents, the majority of them from two nursing homes. The first one that really had the spike was a former county-owned nursing home. My colleagues and I felt terrible about that. Here was a facility that we had sold off about eight years ago and lives were being lost. We received some criticism about that, especially from residents who had lost loved ones, who said that if the county hadn't sold it, this tragedy never would've happened. That really hit me between the eyes because that, obviously, was not our intention. Unfortunately, the problem was that the nursing home had employees coming in with the virus who ended up passing it on to the residents.

Someone I knew, who lost a loved one there, phoned me. He said that he felt the virus was being brought in by outsiders, specifically the staff, which was verified by New York State Department of Health. He described the painful reality that many people were going through, not being able to visit their loved ones. He wasn't the only one who phoned. People were calling me and saying, "I can't visit. I'm frustrated. There are people dying there. Jack, what can you do for us?"

While not as timely and in-depth as I would have liked, the State Department of Health finally intervened and gave the nursing home some guidance. Yet I could easily imagine what families with loved ones in long-term care facilities were going through. A couple of years ago, I'd lost my mother at age ninety. My four siblings and I are thankful that the good Lord took Mom before this pandemic. She had dementia, and it would have been heartbreaking for us not to see her, especially with her not understanding why we couldn't visit. I know that's what many New Yorkers have gone through—that gut-wrenching feeling of having to try and explain why you can't visit, or resorting to standing outside, knocking on the window, and waving.

* * *

From the beginning of the pandemic, my message to county residents has been set politics aside and respect each other, care for one another's health, wear a mask, socially distance, and sanitize your hands. We are going through intense times, and the best way to get through it is together.

As leaders, we are writing history and continue to do so today—now that the vaccine has arrived. If there is any solace for the pain caused by COVID-19 it is this:

Next time, we will be ready.

13

Orange County Executive Steve Neuhaus

I'm a lieutenant commander in the U.S. Navy Reserves who has served in Africa, South Korea, and Iraq. If there is one lesson I have learned from my military experience, it's that the best way to meet an enemy is to be prepared and to organize your people to fight. Here in Orange County, our philosophy comes straight from the military: no one is coming, it's up to us.

In Orange County, we stage regular drills with all hands on deck for any type of apocalypse, from a terrorist attack, to a school shooting, to a nuclear meltdown at a power plant—basically, any type of crisis that can happen. After each exercise, we do a "hot wash," recapping the exercise and reviewing the good, the bad, and the ugly. This training has definitely sharpened our spear. We listen to everyone in the room before we make a decision, so it's never simply a matter of top-down direction. Staff make recommendations, and then I, as the county executive, along with input from my command staff, reject or accept and then implement those recommendations. We move forward as a team.

When COVID-19 hit Orange County, which is comprised of forty-three cities and towns in the Hudson Valley with a population of approximately 385,000, we established a command room at the Emergency Services Center and a daily situation report, or "sitrep," modeled after my briefings in Iraq, was presented. The one-page report provides a facts-only snapshot, including new cases, deaths, hospitalizations, and available resources. The sitrep focuses on capabilities and operational status, answering questions such as "Are we running out of hospital beds?" and "Do we have enough PPE?" I set up a COVID-19 response team, which included myself, the health commissioner, the county attorney, the commissioner of emergency services, and representatives from local hospitals and major medical providers, all of whom were imbedded at the center. I put the deputy county executive in charge of running our usual day-to-day operations and kept in close contact with him. I also spoke regularly with my county department heads and conducted daily calls with the mayors and supervisors across the county.

With the response team in place, we organized a way to communicate with residents to keep them informed and put them at ease. We posted daily videos on social media and the county website, detailing the spread of the virus. The videos received fifteen to twenty thousand views during the worst moments of the pandemic, and five to seven thousand views as things began to improve. The information provided in the briefing videos was delivered in a fresh and honest manner, a direct contrast to Governor Andrew Cuomo and President Donald Trump, whose press conferences were often politically charged and long-winded.

Fortunately, the county had a healthy stockpile of personal protective equipment dating back to the Ebola outbreak, and we had a flexible workforce that was ready, willing, and able to take on various tasks as needed. Our county Office of the Aging was already delivering food to the elderly, so we expanded their program to families who were impacted by unemployment or quarantined. The Public Works Department picked up and delivered PPE whenever and wherever it was needed. Department of Motor Vehicles employees were cross-trained to be contact tracers, and they answered questions about what to do if you tested positive or experienced symptoms of the virus. Economic Development, Tourism and the Office of Employment and Training helped people file for unemployment insurance and loans from the Paycheck Protection Program.

Our PPE came from our own reserves and the federal government. The burn rate was astounding. The county went through 290,000 surgical masks, 200,000 gloves, 189,000 cloth masks, and 120,000 N95 masks. We also went through a huge supply of surgical gowns, face shields, individual hand sanitizers, and goggles. Most of it went to long-term care facilities and nursing homes, which accounted for one-third of our deaths. Then it went to our municipalities, hospitals, community service providers, funeral homes, and daycare centers. We continue to burn through PPE in our hospitals, nursing homes, and medical care facilities.

To help mitigate the economic impact of the pandemic on local businesses, we put together a COVID-19 economic development team to work with small business owners and job seekers to answer their questions and connect them to resources. I also urged the Orange County Funding Corporation to implement a program to offer much-needed low-interest loans to small businesses. We have a close working relationship with the Orange County Chamber of Commerce, and we partnered with it to allow not only its members but also any local businesses to use the county's buying power for their own procurement needs.

In the midst of the crisis, we had to work on our budget, and our sales tax numbers were dismal. Thankfully, we have fewer employees now than we had in 2014, 177 fewer, which saves the county millions of dollars. We also had vacancies that we continue to keep open, which is how we generate our fund balance that will help us to pay our bills and rebuild that fund balance. In addition, early retirement was offered and sixty-four of our employees took advantage of it, which saved us $2 million, and another seventy-nine employees volunteered for furloughs. The furloughs not only saved the county money, but also allowed parents to stay home with their children because the schools were closed. It also allowed employees who had elderly, sick or vulnerable family members to care for them.

One problem counties faced during the pandemic was political. The State Legislature gave Governor Cuomo unilateral control of New York's response to COVID-19, and then left Albany so there was no oversight of the governor. This single point of leadership made it harder for county governments. There was little transparency, and decisions made were unequitable. Big-box stores like Walmart and Home Depot were able to remain open without issue, while Main Street was at first forced to close and then eventually allowed to reopen with reduced staff doing just curbside pickup or with a 50 percent occupancy rate. In my opinion, this was grossly unfair. Going forward through this pandemic or a future pandemic, we need to find a way to keep the economy up and running as much as possible. There are safe ways to keep it going, and our guiding principles should be safety and fairness. Curbside pickup and reduced occupancy are just two of the successful practices that maintained safety but kept businesses up and running.

Despite the social dislocation caused by COVID-19, we discovered new ways to provide a break from the relentless loneliness of isolating from your friends and neighbors. We held a drive-in fireworks display in July and the New York Air Show with an audience of over twelve hundred people in August. At both events, people parked their cars in what from above looked like a giant bingo board. And happily, we had zero COVID-19 positive cases from that event. We also held farmers markets and food trucks, all adapting to the demands of social distancing and masking.

We were able to bring multiple festivals that were canceled throughout the Hudson Valley to Orange County, also using the drive-through and/or drive-in format. Participants picked up their food, and then drove to one of the county's parks, sat in their vehicles, and enjoyed the day. The events, Taco Fest, Empanada Fest, Seafood Fest, and Mac and Cheese Fest, all gave the public something to do, a welcome break from the trials and tribulations of life in the shadow of COVID-19.

So where do we go from here, as we continue through 2021 and COVID remains with us? We hope that the vaccine will be dispensed at a more rapid rate. The initial rollout has been marred with mistakes and failures. A lack of transparency and a micromanaged approach prevented vulnerable populations from getting vaccinated and resulted in unnecessary deaths. There is plenty of grieving and sadness, but there is also an abundance of hope. Overall, I am proud of how we have handled this unprecedented pandemic, and proud of what we accomplished here in Orange County, the families that we have assisted and the lives we have touched and saved.

As a county, we will remain vigilant and see ourselves through this pandemic, and whatever challenges the future may hold.

14

Putnam County Executive MaryEllen Odell

As soon as we learned that a New Rochelle lawyer, the first patient in the state hospitalized with COVID-19, was a commuter on Metro-North Railroad, I knew we had to get ready. Putnam County residents are among the thousands of people who commute daily through Grand Central Station, and odds favored that some of them would bring the virus home.

We couldn't protect our residents without a functioning Emergency Services Center, so I called Ken Clair Jr., the commissioner of that department, and asked him to lock down the facility. I didn't want anyone entering the building without a temperature check. We wanted everyone logged in and logged out if we had to track an infection. Obviously, the center is critical to public safety regardless of the emergency.

Next up was to put the right people in the room and to start talking to our colleagues throughout the Hudson Valley to learn what we were facing. The right people were from the health department, emergency services, the county attorney, and the commissioner of finance.

It was clear that the elderly were most vulnerable to the virus, and one of our first decisions was to close our senior centers, where people gathered and ate lunch every day. Michael Cunningham, our director of senior services, quickly came up with a plan to home-deliver their meals. We thought we'd open up the centers in a couple weeks.

On March 13, I issued my first executive order after the school superintendents from Putnam/Northern Westchester BOCES asked us to close the schools to protect teachers, students, and their families. We had consulted with counsel and with Marc Molinaro, the Dutchess County executive. Marc was getting the same request from his school superintendents and planning to issue his own order to close. In our announcement, we were careful not to incite panic and characterized the decision as a reasonable precaution.

Governor Andrew Cuomo had not yet ordered school closings statewide, and on the afternoon of my announcement the governor's office called to inform us that we had overstepped our authority. Our county attorney, Jennifer Bumgarner, and I spoke to the governor's counsel, saying that we had no intention of usurping the governor's authority, but we had a request from the stakeholders, and I consulted with experts in our health department and based our decision on professional advice.

That weekend, I issued three more executive orders—putting a halt to buffets in restaurants and markets, limiting gatherings to twenty people, and closing all state-regulated daycare facilities. Again, I made the decision after consulting with counsel and experts, and again I drew the governor's ire. His lawyers called. Governor Cuomo wanted to keep the daycare centers open so that essential workers could get to their jobs. I understood the reasoning, but it seemed inconsistent with the governor's own call to close the schools, which he had made by then. Anyway, I agreed to rescind the daycare order.

The terrible human cost of COVID-19 hit home for me when Robert Shannon, a dispatcher in our 911 call center, died. Dispatcher Shannon was forty-nine, and he was our first experience of losing a co-worker to the virus, and it was a shock. He hadn't been infected at the Emergency Operation Center, but we immediately quarantined anyone who had been in contact with him, and we had the building sanitized again. Luckily, the virus didn't spread through dispatch. But we lost a good man.

* * *

In the first weeks of the pandemic, the biggest challenge we faced was acquiring the appropriate amount of testing kits. (We are doing better now, and because we have good relations with our neighboring counties—Rockland,

Dutchess, and Orange—we could create a consortium and buy personal protective equipment in bulk at a good price.) Besides getting our hands on the necessary equipment, we were consumed with managing the shutdown and setting up a communication network for department heads, the county legislature, the media, and the public. We reiterated the message that the public health professionals had taught us: wear masks, socially distance, wash your hands often, and stay home as much as you can.

The three crucial takeaways for me were communicate, communicate, and communicate. My team would be on the phone from morning until night, sharing information. We created a dashboard, which outlined all the information we had. Later, we studied surrounding counties' dashboards and incorporated their ideas. That dashboard was an efficient way to pass along the data our residents needed. Legislators routinely posted it on Facebook; we posted it on our website and sent it to the media. In our war against COVID-19, information was among our most effective weapons.

As we began to make headway, we had time to think about the impact of the business closings on us. We were getting executive orders from the governor's office daily: shut this down, shut that down. Most businesses were confused as to what was permitted. They were constantly calling our office, and I couldn't blame them. We are a Main Street economy, so we know who we are talking to when they are on the other end of the line. We had business owners who lost their income; landlords who weren't collecting rent; and residents on unemployment.

We knew that we would have to do something to jumpstart the economy once we were allowed to reopen. We were fortunate to have a very professional president of the Economic Development Corporation, Kathleen Abels; we had also just brought on a new director of tourism, Tracey Walsh; and I moved now Deputy County Executive Tom Feighery from his public works projects to help. Tom has been a business owner for thirty-five years, and he's recognized as a great ally of so many different organizations in the county.

We planned our reopening which would begin when the governor allowed us to enter Phase 1. I was feeling optimistic until the Saturday before Memorial Day when, on a conference call along with my colleagues from the Hudson Valley, the governor informed us that if we didn't train ninety contract tracers by Monday, we wouldn't be able to enter Phase 1 on Tuesday.

We spent the rest of the weekend making frantic calls, trying to get ninety people to agree to interrupt their holiday weekend to take an eight-hour training course in contact tracing. I'm still amazed that we did it, and on Tuesday, May 26, our reopening began.

The one business that thrived during the first wave of the pandemic was golf. I took so much heat for keeping the Putnam County Golf Course open, but everyone who could wanted to play golf. It was a way to get outside, see your friends, and stay at a safe distance. In 2020, the golf course set a record for the most rounds ever played.

* * *

Throughout all of this, seven days a week, we had our afternoon call with the governor's office. That was our portal to getting our questions answered. We are still required to participate in the daily call, though no longer on weekends. Now the information centers on outbreaks and clusters. Fortunately, Putnam has been spared from most of that. Infections in the schools are low, and the superintendents immediately address them. The county had a small cluster back in July. For several months, we had no deaths: we were holding steady at sixty-three; it was sixty-seven by the New Year. We're not sure all of the deceased were our residents. Some patients had come up to Putnam Hospital from Westchester and New York City. Not that it matters. Each loss was a sorrow beyond words.

Our most serious lack of communication from the governor's office concerned our unpaid reimbursements and the threat that the governor would withhold from 20 to 50 percent of our state aid, which has made it impossible for us to plan. Our sales tax numbers were good, but we will have to see if that holds. We take a conservative approach to projecting revenue, so we can bring in our budget under the tax cap and not have layoffs and not have to go back to the unions and ask for a freeze—a problem that has beset some of our colleagues in other counties.

By no means are we out of the woods. Unemployment is higher in the county than it's ever been. If there is a recession in 2021, we have no idea if it will be short or long. The future is murkier than ever. Our government has been operating with half its normal staff. And we still have services to deliver to our residents—meals for the homebound, help for veterans, social services for those in need, roads that have to be repaired. We have a very high senior population, and I've been worried about their mental and physical well-being. We've lost a number of seniors, and I'm certain that the isolation and lack of activities that we usually offer them took its toll. This has been particularly hard for me. Whenever I read the obituaries of our seniors, I pray that it wasn't because they were lonely and isolated in the last months of their lives.

In some ways, the second wave has been harder on us. We've lost more friends and loved ones. At the same time, COVID fatigue has spread as quickly as the virus. People want to visit friends and family and get back to business. Parents are trying to manage their work schedule, while raising and teaching their children, all without help from grandparents and neighbors.

I remember first hearing of the coronavirus outbreak on the news when it was in China. It seemed distant. There had been other dangerous virus outbreaks in recent years, but none of them affected us. I assumed this would be the same. This pandemic has been an education for all of us, hasn't it?

Now that the vaccine is available, we will, in time, put

this virus behind us. The tragedies will be with some of us forever. Yet if COVID-19 has taught us anything, it is what people can accomplish if they pull in the same direction. In the midst of our sadness, we have seen acts of heroism and compassion and selflessness. I saw it in our county employees, who never failed to rise to the occasion, and for that, I am both proud and eternally grateful.

15

Rensselaer County Executive Steven McLaughlin

In mid-March, around St. Patrick's Day, I was in Washington, D.C., with Albany County Executive Dan McCoy when I learned that Rensselaer County had logged its first positive case of COVID-19. No luck of the Irish that day.

I came home to bedlam, and it didn't help that we were in the midst of the nasty 2020 presidential campaign. Daily on TV, Governor Andrew Cuomo screamed at President Donald Trump as if the president was supposed to be a communicable-disease expert. It was a circus. The fact is, only one question was important: how fast can we contain the virus?

I'd been an airline pilot. You're trained to handle emergencies—to aviate, navigate, and communicate. I applied this approach. Aviate would be you fly the plane.

You don't panic, you just do your job. In the case of COVID-19, you make sure that the county keeps going. Then you navigate. How do we find our way through this? And finally, you communicate—this is where we need to be, and this is how we'll get there.

From watching the tragic outcomes in nursing homes in Seattle, I saw that we had to protect the residents in Van Rensselaer Manor, our county-owned nursing home. So, on March 25, when Governor Cuomo directed nursing homes to accept patients who had or were suspected of having COVID-19, I refused to comply. I don't believe that you blindly go along because a governor had someone write an order on a piece of paper if, in your heart, you know it's wrong. We tested everyone before admitting them. That should've been done everywhere. You can't introduce a virus to a frail population and then be shocked by the awful outcome.

Still, the virus is an invisible enemy, and you can't always keep it out, particularly when staff members, who were asymptomatic, bring it in the door. Many of the workers were part-time and worked at other facilities, so we immediately put a stop to that. We had our staff agree that they wouldn't work at any other nursing homes and offered them more hours so they wouldn't lose money, and we fired a few people who continued to work elsewhere.

We also sanitized the Manor with an aqueous-chloride solution applied with a pressure washer. It goes on almost dry and then is electrostatically charged. It's an extremely expensive two-step process, but worth it because it provides an operating-room level of clean that lasts for three months. We did the same sanitizing at a local hotel where we were housing the homeless population who had contracted the virus.

I butted heads with the state again when I wouldn't let their inspectors into our nursing home because we couldn't verify that they weren't infected, and the state refused to provide proof that they had been tested. At last, after we objected to two inspections, the state relented and provided a letter saying inspectors were being tested. Common sense prevailed, but it was too long in coming. Dealing with the state and testing had been a nuisance from the start. Securing test sites from them was like pulling teeth, so we did it ourselves.

Over the summer, we opened up outdoor, socially distanced visitation for the residents. There was a plastic-like shower curtain between them, and they were six feet apart and people were wearing masks and sanitizing. We did this because we know that loneliness and isolation from loved ones can kill the elderly. It's an approach we continue to press with the state—that we have to find a way for these families to see each other. If the state is going to tell us that masks and social distancing work, then let's take the next step.

I was gratified by the emails, phone calls, tweets, and Facebook posts that I and my staff received thanking us for protecting Mom and Dad and Grandma and Grandpa. I know many of the folks in Van Rensselaer Manor, and I know their families. And I knew how hard the losses could be. An old friend of mine died from the virus. For me, refusing to comply with the governor's irresponsible directive was a matter of conscience. Yet despite all of our caution, our nursing home lost three residents. I was distraught, though I knew it could've been far worse. Small comfort, but I did everything in my power to protect our residents, and that continues every day.

We were also very concerned about the ability of Samaritan Hospital to handle a rush of patients. Every day, they were getting folks from New York City coming up by helicopter. We were worried about the shortage of personal protective equipment, and at one point Governor Cuomo threatened to take our ventilators by force. Thankfully, that didn't happen. Our nurses, doctors, paramedics, police, and firefighters were in the middle of it all, and we kept hearing stories about them reusing masks and gowns, and we addressed that as quickly as we could. That's still an everyday issue for us, and I find myself checking on our supply of PPE on a daily basis.

It would be bad enough if COVID-19 was just a healthcare challenge. It isn't. In Rensselaer County, for much of the pandemic, we'd lost more people to drug overdoses than to the virus, and you can't turn a blind eye to folks who are so depressed and not getting the services they need that they wind up dead from drugs. We've had to beef up our outreach to this population. We literally are delivering Narcan door-to-door, no questions asked, to whomever might need it. And on top of everything, we're watching businesses fail. People who put their life savings on the line are being shut down, and they worry about feeding their families, and to see the fear in their eyes is devastating. It's been tough to balance: keeping everybody safe while understanding that a failing economy is also dangerous.

Owners of bars, restaurants, yoga studios, gyms, and movie theaters have been reaching out for help, telling me that they have no idea how they are going to save their businesses. A real point of frustration for them was the constantly changing phases of reopening. We would be within a day of Phase 2, and the governor and his team would yank the rug out from under us. They'd tell us that we can't reopen in the Capital Region because our hospitalization rate was too high. They didn't know what they were talking about. All the county executives know the numbers in their counties, and we know that Governor Cuomo has a strange method for counting. If you live in Albany, but happen to be hospitalized at Samaritan in Troy, that infection is counted against Rensselaer County. If you live in Troy and are a patient at Albany Medical Center, that goes on the Albany County side of the ledger. It's ridiculous that at this late date the state continues to get this wrong, and county executives have been calling to complain about it.

When you own a business that is on the verge of disappearing and you've been shut down for months, every day you're delayed from reopening is a catastrophe. It frustrated me to no end, and we decided that if your business did not require a state license to operate—bars and barber shops, for instance—then you could open up. I had so many owners reaching out to tell me that we saved them from ruin. It has worked out fine. You have to trust people to be smart about their reopening, and that is what we did. And in Rensselaer County our folks have done a great job. It never made any sense to me why you could have a thousand people at a Walmart or Target, but you couldn't have local stores opening when mom-and-pop businesses have far less ability to withstand a downturn.

When it comes to the financial situation of our county, fears remain. Somehow, in the greatest economy anybody alive had ever seen, the state has run into a multibillion-dollar deficit. Pre-COVID, it was $6 billion, so the state had significant issues prior to January. These significant structural issues with the state budget always flow downhill to the counties, cities, and towns. That's a huge worry for us because there seems to be no idea or plan at the state level other than hoping for a federal bailout. Hope isn't a plan, and if you fail to plan, you're going to be in serious trouble.

The state is already withholding money from counties, which is a problem and no surprise. The upside for Rensselaer County is that we're growing our businesses. Last year, we had the best sales tax revenue growth in the state. I believe all the counties were up, on average, about 4.2 percent. We were up over 8 percent and we banked a lot of that money, adding $15 million to our surplus knowing full well—though I didn't know it would be this bad—that rainy days invariably come.

I'm always optimistic—I consider it part of my job—but my natural optimism is tempered by the unfortunate fact that I don't know what the state has planned for the counties, and it's not helpful that the Cuomo administration is not forthcoming with information. Since the crisis began, the governor has only addressed the county executives once, and it was a lecture on everything that we needed to do instead of a conversation about what we were seeing, and how the state might help if we all worked in a more collaborative way.

Communication is key. We do Zoom calls with our school superintendents every week. We set aside about an hour to answer any of their questions. We ask what they need and how we can help. We can't solve every problem immediately—a new standard in the time of Twitter—but creating the sense that we are all pulling in the same direction helps. Which is why I do a weekly Facebook Live broadcast. To let people know I'm out there trying—that someone cares about their struggles.

In retrospect, I'm not sure what I would've done differently. Maybe I should have kept a daily journal. There's still time, I suppose. We're not through this yet.

I may be the top of the pyramid, but there are so many people in our county who have done so much to help. And the public has held up its end, doing what they needed to do to keep themselves and their neighbors safe. We say to them, "Listen, you're American citizens, you're free. We are not going to be overly restrictive; we are not going to be jumping all over you. Here's what we are asking everybody to do."

So we have had very few complaints. The public gets it, thank God, and they deserve a lot of credit.

In the end, all we can do is try to go about our lives as best we can, knowing that here, in this country, we have confronted worse situations throughout our history, and we endured.

That's our goal—to endure.

16

Rockland County Executive Ed Day

I first became aware of COVID-19 in February 2020. At the time, no one seemed to think it was going to be any worse in the United States than the flu. In San Francisco, people were encouraged to go out and celebrate the Chinese New Year. In fact, the general attitude from elected officials was that COVID-19 was nothing to worry about. As a former commanding officer of detective squads in the Bronx and the chief of detectives of the Baltimore Police Department, I'm hardly Pollyannaish about human nature. But it's amazing to me how these officials could make those statements and then later not take ownership of them. Everybody's entitled to make a mistake. However, it becomes a problem when officials are more concerned about their reputations than what's happening on the ground, and the problem is that people will no longer trust you and fear will spread. And in dealing with a pandemic, and the dislocation it causes and the necessity of government interfering with normal life, trust is the key to leadership.

On March 14, our medical examiner confirmed the first local COVID-19 death, and tragically it was the first of many. (By mid-February 2021, we were approaching seven hundred deaths, once an inconceivable number but now a number that troubles me beyond description.) Rockland has a population of approximately 325,000, and many of our residents commute to New York City, where infections were rampant. It was a déjà vu moment for us because we'd had a similar situation the year before with measles outbreak, but COVID-19 was proving to be far deadlier, and we realized that we had to make major changes to the way we operated.

We declared a local state of emergency and closed the schools, and subsequent to that Governor Andrew Cuomo issued his own orders. Handling the pandemic felt very much like police work in that there was a need to immediately pivot and take action. I'd been to countless crime scenes as a police commander where multiple people were shot, and everyone is looking at you to be the voice of calm and to give direction. In my office, I have the Rudyard Kipling poem "If" on a wall. The opening lines—"If you can keep your head when all about you are losing theirs"—sums up my management philosophy.

After our first death, I was most afraid that we didn't know what we were facing. Lack of knowledge about an adversary frightens people. I had that concern. We had a rapidly evolving situation, and the rules were changing day to day. That was problematic from my perspective, so we charted our own way. We canceled events and announced public exposures. A background in law enforcement will give you an almost religious belief in the importance of organization. The same is true of the military, and my deputy county executive is a retired lieutenant colonel; my chief of staff is a retired lieutenant colonel; and at the fire training center we have another retired lieutenant colonel. We all bring different skill sets to the table, but we all believe in a mission-oriented approach to solving problems.

When it came to organizing how we would communicate with our residents, we used every channel available. We used Facebook Live to answer residents' questions, put up a link to that on YouTube, and sent it out in an email blast. The most critical piece that you need when communicating during a crisis is believability. If you don't have that, you've already lost the war. I always tried to be careful in my comments and as factual as possible. If I didn't know something, I said that I didn't know it. You can't be ashamed to do that. Ignorance is talking out of turn. I wish that our politicians and experts would weigh their words before they speak, because everything said is being scrutinized. Throughout the country, we have a very anxious population, particularly in New York. And words count.

* * *

From personal experience, I knew that COVID-19 was serious business. Some friends and acquaintances of mine passed away from the virus. My nephew, an officer with the New York City Police Department, contracted it. He recovered easily, but my son Michael, a Green Beret, was hit hard by it, as was his wife, a twenty-four-year-old athletic trainer. For me, then, this notion that COVID-19 is only a problem for older people and those with comorbidities doesn't compute. Thankfully, my family members are feeling better, though my concern as a dad and an uncle is that we still don't know the long-term effects of the virus once the initial symptoms recede. This pandemic is a learning experience, and, at the moment, there are questions without answers.

From the beginning, I thought it was wise to proceed with caution—masks, social distancing, frequent hand washing. However, in Rockland there were communities who didn't want to follow the public health orders for political or religious reasons. Resistance to being told what to do transcends communities. By and large, most people will complain about being inconvenienced regardless of their backgrounds.

We had to rely on the leaders in our large Hasidic community to tackle the restrictions associated with the COVID-19 orders. We used the same back-channel communication to the rabbis who trusted us from our work during the measles epidemic. Understandably, in light of the Holocaust, many Hasidim are apprehensive about directives from government, and the community is insular by tradition. They have outliers who wouldn't listen to the rabbis and refused to follow the rules. We did everything reasonably possible to get them to do so. We had a few instances where we had to fine people. Once that happened, it didn't really happen again. We'd made our point.

With our residents getting sick and dying, it seemed almost obscene to worry about money, but that is the job of a county executive—how to pay the bills through good years and bad. I'd been a part-time legislator during the 2008 recession, so when I saw what was happening during the pandemic, I told myself that I'd seen this movie before, and it was going to have a better ending.

We took immediate action in March. We implemented a hiring freeze, filed for FEMA reimbursements, and abolished all vacant government positions, which saved us about $2 million. Then I asked, "What are we not doing because of the pandemic?" The answer was about $8 million worth of events. So we saved that money, but even that wasn't enough. We still had to help the poor and elderly and perform the tasks the state requires of county government. In July, we found out that the sales tax revenue was down 50 percent. That was catastrophic. Our total budget is a little over $700 million, so it was a significant hit. To combat that, we met with the county legislature in August and charted out a course of action. My proposed 2022 austerity budget went in on October 1. During this time, I was speaking to all of my colleagues in the Mid-Hudson region, seeking any idea that would help, and for now we have been able to mitigate the financial damage.

* * *

At the local government level, my experience has been that, yes, political conflict between Democrats and Republicans is unavoidable, but by and large when faced with COVID-19, most of what goes on is cooperative in nature, and politics has been set aside.

Unfortunately, at the higher levels of government, it seemed that leaders were more concerned about political issues than the good of the people. That was evident with some of the confusing reopenings, and this not only devastated businesses, but undermined the credibility of government.

By all accounts, the vaccine rollout has been chaotic. There is no other way to describe it. There are things Governor Andrew Cuomo is doing now that should have been done in December, when we submitted our vaccine plan. During the measles epidemic we had administered over thirty thousand vaccines in Rockland County. We had the local health departments trained and kept the measles-free designation for the entire county and did it with five days to spare despite being the most impacted county in the nation. We came out of that strong so I was ready for us to vaccinate Rockland County again. We could do a minimum of four hundred a day and had done upwards of seven hundred in one day. Our health department is housed in a former hospital/nursing home, so we had an excellent setup, and we were prepared. The trouble was that we couldn't get our hands on enough doses to take care of our residents.

Looking back, I'm proud of our ability to organize during the pandemic, and that pride is twofold. One is in knowing that you can count on the people working with you—the local governments, middle management, and commissioners. The second is seeing the positive reaction of the residents, the people you are duty-bound to help and protect. I went up to the health department when they were immunizing some of our seniors, and people came up to me and couldn't have been more thankful. As scared as they were, they wanted to hug me. It was gratifying because leaders dealing with emergencies can either panic and run or they can band together and get something done.

We did the latter, and I will be proud of that until the end of my days.

17

Suffolk County Executive Steven Bellone

It was not too long after the first confirmed case of COVID-19 in Suffolk County that we realized we had a crisis on our hands. Less than a week after March 9, 2020, the circumstances became dire. Facing an unprecedented public health emergency, I declared a state of emergency. Terms such as "social distancing" and "hot zones" may have been new to the national lexicon, but Suffolk County, the largest county in New York, overnight found itself as the epicenter of a global pandemic.

When I heard that the first positive case to impact our county workforce was my chief deputy county executive, everything changed in an instant. The prognosis forced our entire senior staff to quarantine, diverting our core command into remote and unchartered territory. For me, it was a recognition that I needed to manage my communications response differently as I complied with the guidance set forth by the state.

In a sense, we were fortunate. New technologies would emerge and prove vital when we needed them most. While I had never heard of Zoom, I began to use this new platform regularly for daily media briefings from my home office in the early days of the pandemic. For more than one hundred consecutive days thereafter, we continued those briefings. It also synced with other online or social media platforms, creating a unique opportunity to speak directly to my constituents at a time when they needed to hear from their county executive. It also afforded the opportunity to create our own programming by having others join me to discuss the topic of the day.

In the early stages of the crisis, the routine was simple—early morning televised briefings with national cable outlets to explain to other parts of the country what was heading their way. After dealing with any technical issues from the producers, I was speaking to a televised audience from the chair in my office.

By April, Suffolk County surpassed one thousand deaths, with more cases on Long Island than any state other than New York or New Jersey. The situation was growing worse. The numbers were not flattening in Suffolk County as they were in New York City, but rather accelerating. The number of confirmed cases in Suffolk County was rising by one thousand per day, then fifteen hundred cases, with no end in sight.

The human toll was unavoidable, though we recognized

that our best chance to obtain more resources from the federal government was by showing powerful imagery on the ground. We called television stations and anyone who would hear our story, using behind-the-scenes access when possible. When we were forced to transform our county farm into a makeshift morgue because of capacity constraints, MSNBC was there on the scene.

This problem was compounded by the shortage of PPE. There simply were not enough gowns, gloves, face shields, ear loop masks, and N95 masks to shield doctors and nurses from this highly contagious virus. I made the case to Brian Kilmeade one morning on Fox News as I held up the front cover of Newsday with an infamous headline that said nurses were using plastic garbage bags as makeshift gowns. I knew that our public engagement and lobbying behind the scenes were finally beginning to pay off. Shortly after we made an emergency request to distribute supplies to our hospitals, President Donald Trump announced that the White House would airdrop a shipment of two hundred thousand N95 masks to Suffolk County. It came at an opportune time when our ICU bed capacity and hospitalizations were continuing to rise.

Then there was the financial impact of this crisis as well. The virus effectively shut down our national economy, and overnight store fronts were closed for business. In the short term, we needed to help small business owners readjust for the new reality. We recognized that people received their information not only from traditional media outlets but social media and government websites, too.

We responded by standing up a Business Recovery Unit website to assist small businesses and leveraged our 311 call center to relay information in real time. We then went further. In May, we announced Suffolk Forward, a package of five programs in partnership with Stony Brook University designed to help local businesses adjust and respond to the new business climate. Since the pandemic exposed just how many small businesses lacked the technology capabilities to transition to virtual or online services, we leveraged expertise to improve their IT infrastructure.

In many ways, this was a state-by-state response. In many ways, it was localized. I held daily briefing calls with town and village officials to make sure they had what they needed and could relay important information to their constituents on the latest state guidance. There were still a significant number of residents that relied on their local governments to see to it that they had everything they needed. If it was meals for seniors, they knew who to contact in their town. New partnerships emerged among counties. When Governor Cuomo established a Downstate NY Reopening Task Force, every decision about opening beaches to pools were made in consideration of each other.

Irrespective of the traditional upstate-downstate divide, the devastation that this pandemic wrought threw the old playbook out the window. Instead of pitting one against the other, county executives formed a united front, using one voice to amplify an urgent message on the need for Washington to deliver federal disaster assistance. Soon we were organizing weekly Zoom media updates with other county executives to touch nearly every corner of the state. Our strategy was to target media markets with members of Congress that represented traditional swing districts. In an election year, federal relief was the best leverage we had to make it clear that jobs and livelihoods were on the line.

I believe the pandemic has made us more resilient and will make us stronger in the long term. As county executives, this pandemic forced us to work together to meet challenges that we could not handle alone. I think of my colleague Onondaga County Executive Ryan McMahon, who graciously dispatched nurses from Upstate University Hospital in Syracuse to help us deal with our hospitalizations. It was a recognition that we are one New York. I think this experience has shown us how we can learn from each other and find common ground even during a politically polarized time.

18

Ulster County Executive Patrick Ryan

Ulster County sits outside the suburban ring of New York City. We were just far enough away that as COVID-19 began to spread we didn't receive the same resources as the city and Westchester. However, a significant number of our one hundred seventy-eight thousand residents commute to work in the city or maintain close ties with friends and family there, so I felt it was critical for us to get a data-driven picture of what was happening in our county.

In the weeks leading up to our first positive case on March 8, we held a series of tabletop exercises to plan everything from logistics to setting up mass quarantines to what we would do if an outbreak occurred at a school. On March 11, we converted our conference room at the department of health into a call center with 911 operators, county employees, public health nurses, and volunteers. To start, the hotline operated ten hours a day, seven days a week.

In the conference room, we set up a board and tracked our cases. We were getting hundreds of calls a day. This was also an effective way to push out information and reassure our residents that a real-live human being cared about their situation and would try to answer their questions. This was especially important to our homebound seniors and anyone else who was struggling. Before long, we had reached thirty thousand calls, and over time we shifted from COVID health calls to "I need food" and "I need shelter" calls, or I'm having a mental health crisis. We tracked our response time and tried to make sure everyone received help.

On March 12, four days after our first positive case, I declared a state of emergency, suspended in-person county services, and created a Health and Safety Task Force to advise the county on its response to the virus. The next day, in coordination with school superintendents, we closed our schools. Initially, the closure was slated for two weeks, but as the infection rate jumped, we went to remote instruction for the rest of the school year.

That weekend, I held a telephone town hall with our county health commissioner that drew over ten thousand participants. While we only had five positives in the county, interest among residents was high, and our office went to great lengths to communicate with the public on these issues. Teaming up with a local radio station, we hosted a near-daily Facebook Live town hall, which was simulcast in Spanish and with an interpreter for our hearing-impaired residents. In over fifty town halls, we took dozens of live questions, and we were joined by two statewide office holders, our member of Congress, state legislators, and health professionals.

In mid-March, we launched Project Resilience, and in a single day we raised $2 million, mobilized hundreds of volunteers, and signed up over a hundred local restaurants to prepare meals. Over the next four months, we delivered nearly three hundred thousand meals, kept dozens of restaurants open and hundreds employed. While communities across the country were witnessing long lines of cars waiting for food, we were delivering food to peoples' doorsteps.

A week later, we opened a county-run drive-through testing clinic by partnering with Nuvance Health. In the days following we were able to open a total of three county-operated testing facilities, including a walk-in facility in the city of Kingston so we could reach the underprivileged.

Before the end of the month, we held our Small Business Webinar, which was attended by over four hundred business owners. In the first round of the Paycheck Protection Program loan distribution, we were able to help our businesses obtain over $120 million in funding. With a $100,000 investment by Ulster County Economic Development Alliance, we assisted women and minority-owned businesses, along with businesses in low and moderate-income census tracts, to become eligible for $2 million in loan funding. The monies were targeted at stabilizing small businesses and nonprofits.

On April 6, after a weekend that saw our hospitalization rates increase by 50 percent, we issued a public warning that, at our current pace, both hospital space and ventilators would soon be exhausted. By the end of that week, we were able to double our capacity of ventilators. We transformed the Kate Walton Field House on the Kingston High School campus into a surge medical treatment facility. We then started work at TechCity, a former IBM building that the county had obtained through foreclosure, building out one hundred thousand square feet for use as a potential hospital.

In the first days of the pandemic, seeing a shortage of personal protective equipment, we were forced to purchase PPE from China. However, through a partnership with SUNY New Paltz's Advanced Manufacturing Center, we were able to produce and distribute tens of thousands of face shields to local governments and healthcare providers. We teamed up with a local distiller and produced our own hand sanitizer.

Then, too, we tackled issues that were not health related. Our Tenant Protection Hotline, staffed by members of the Ulster County Public Defender's Office, made sure tenants' rights were protected. The Ulster County Resilience Economic Initiative coordinated our economic development efforts with three main lines of effort—recover, reopen, and realign. Our Recovery Task Force ensured a coordinated and compassionate response to the devastating socioeconomic impacts of the pandemic on our residents. Ulster County saw a surge in SNAP applications, senior meals on wheels requests, and many other key services, and the task force worked to develop new ways to deliver critical services.

These efforts led us to take a hard look at the housing shortage that we face in the county—ironically and sadly, many of our first responders couldn't afford to live in the community where they were literally saving lives. Teaming up with the county legislature, we formed the Housing Advisory Committee and began inventorying county-owned properties for future housing use, eventually identifying the property where the county jail had once stood as a future home for workforce housing.

In late April, we started our own Rapid Response Team and sent our health department with PPE and testing kits to test all thirteen of the nursing homes in the county. Without a doubt, this saved lives.

We started to see a decrease in positive cases, and by the end of May, we entered Phase 1 reopening. Then, during the summer, infections spiked across the country, and we implemented a plan that focused on identifying cases by testing, investigating through contact tracing, isolating through quarantines, communicating by keeping the public informed, and continuing to enforce the PAUSE order. We also launched an "Ulster County Get Tested Week." By then, we had already tested roughly fifty thousand residents.

In anticipation of residents wanting to celebrate July Fourth, and with all regional events canceled, we organized our own "Independence Day Weekend Salute to Essential Workers." We organized parades and cavalcades around the county, recognizing individuals who had gone above and beyond over the last few months, and we concluded with a socially distanced drive-through fireworks display.

In addition, along with the Ulster County Chamber of Commerce, we created our own drive-through movie theater. With a capacity of two hundred cars, we showed films from *Star Wars* to *Frozen* during the summer. Both the Fourth of July event and the movies are not in the traditional purview of government, but we felt it was essential to offer residents some sense of normalcy.

While New York State cleared schools for in-person learning, nearly all of our schools opted to operate initially online or in a hybrid approach. Realizing the strain that this would cause many parents, we launched our Project Resilience Child Care Initiative. We utilized $200,000 in funding to expand existing programs provided by the county as well as giving families the ability to participate with their children.

Tragically, in the six months following the outbreak of COVID-19, we saw a 90 percent increase in opioid-related overdoses. I declared a public health emergency and signed an executive order that placed Narcan kits in high-risk locations. In addition, the first initiative of my 2021 Executive Budget, was a commitment to dedicate over $670,000 to opioid-use prevention.

Naturally, stabilizing our finances was a priority. Our finance department estimated that we could be dealing with a $34 million shortfall. I'm glad to say that we delivered a budget that held the line on taxes, proposed no layoffs, and improved our delivery of vital services.

By the New Year, 6,530 people in the county were infected, and we had tragically lost 157 of our residents. We did everything we could think of to stop the virus, and while I know we did an outstanding job and worked as hard as we could, the losses stay with you longer than the triumphs.

Now, we await the vaccine, and our chance to address the economic and human consequences of the pandemic.

I am eager to do both.

We continue to remain proactive and prepare for the next challenges we may face. We are finalizing our plan to implement a countywide rapid testing capability, conducting initial planning for vaccine distribution, and refining our Rapid Response plans for schools, senior facilities, and other high-risk entities. We know that we have more challenges ahead, both in terms of the COVID pandemic and the resulting socioeconomic impact, but we stand ready to guide our community's response during this unprecedented moment.

19

Westchester County Executive George Latimer

Lately, I've been remembering the way my parents described their experiences during the Great Depression and World War II. When they were telling me these stories, I was a teenager and not interested in hearing tales of yesteryear. Now, I think back to what my parents told me—the sacrifices they made, how leaders at that time were forced to come up with answers that weren't clearly presented to them—and I believe that COVID-19 is our test, our call to do what needs to be done.

In a recent State of the County message, I asked: "Are we fierce? Do we have the mindset that will not let us buckle under an obstacle?"

I believe we do. The cartoon picture of Westchester—a suburban county where our nearly one million residents are extremely wealthy—is a misrepresentation. We are a diverse county with people from different cultural backgrounds and parts of the world. Some are new to the community; others have lived here all their lives. And they are distributed across the economic spectrum, with 8.4 percent living in poverty.

Our first case of COVID-19 was in New Rochelle at the end of February 2019. An individual who had attended a bar mitzvah and a funeral wound up in the hospital and tested positive for the virus. Prior to his diagnosis, he had infected a number of other people in his congregation. Our department of health went to work, doing the contact tracing and the field testing. When we learned the extent of the infections, I met with Governor Andrew Cuomo, Benjamin Boykin, chairman of the Westchester County Board of Legislators, and a host of healthcare and Jewish leaders.

That led the governor to create a zone within this one area of New Rochelle where there was a concentration of potential exposures. There were three schools within the New Rochelle School District, three schools in the Tuckahoe School District, and a number of houses of worship. Back then, all we had was the in-home testing. We maxed at about one hundred tests a day. In fairly short order, it was clear that our folks were being pushed beyond their ability, and at one point the state stepped in to administer the tests.

Soon enough, we had a queue of almost three thousand people who needed to be tested. These were people who felt sick, stayed home, and called their doctor. Or maybe they went to see the doctor, properly protected, and the doctor instructed them to get a COVID test. We also had firefighters, police, and EMS personnel who had responded to calls and dealt with people who had been infected. This happened with three of our police officers who administered Narcan to a woman. Coming out of her overdose, she said, "You know, I may have COVID."

Understandably, we were inundated with requests for a mobile testing site. One was set up in a parking lot of a county park in Glen Island, and a couple of days later another was set up by the state in partnership with Northwell Health. By March 19, we had eight hundred positive cases, 20 percent of the total in New York State. The rate of the spread was stunning. It didn't mean that everyone became seriously ill, but we had to figure out how to isolate thousands of people.

In an earlier incarnation, I was a marketing executive, and if I knew one thing to be true, it was the importance of communication. As county executive I'd been using Facebook Live multiple times a week. You could see all of my press conferences there, so even before COVID-19 hit us, I had a strong social-media presence.

When the pandemic started, we did a news conference right away. From then on, it became a daily occurrence. Even when the governor began his briefings, I still appeared in front of the media every day. I did this because I was convinced that it was the best way to give residents a local view, while reassuring them that we were doing everything we could think of, and then doing something in addition to that.

We had Michael Orth, our director of mental health, come on to talk about the different strategies for staying calm and looking after your emotional well-being. And because the schools were closed, I did a video talking to the schoolchildren of the county, and read them a book.

While the county had regular conference calls with all of our municipal governments and school superintendents, I personally stayed in touch with each of our forty-five different city councils, village boards, and town boards. Some of the meetings took place over Zoom, others were in the chamber where everyone socially distanced and wore masks. Long ago, I discovered, nothing helps people more in a difficult situation than being listened to.

I also scheduled group calls with hospital administrators, representatives from our local nonprofits, the county government unions' group and union leaders. I'm not saying that what we're doing is earthshaking or anything that no one's done before. Even so, it should be done if you want to keep everyone pulling in the same direction to beat back the pandemic.

The fact is that when it comes to responding to emergencies, the logistics of it rarely create the headline-grabbing enthusiasm that the heroic actions of doctors, nurses, law enforcement, or other frontline workers do. But for those heroes to do their jobs, they need to be provided with the supplies and other resources that make it possible for them to serve us, and the county plays a crucial role in making that happen.

In a matter of days, Westchester County became the

East Coast epicenter of the virus. Since then, we have worked relentlessly to provide the resources necessary to keep our citizens safe, and provide first responders with the tools they need to do their jobs.

In retrospect, I'm still amazed at how suddenly the crisis ballooned and surpassed our healthcare system's ability to deal with the sick and those in need of testing. As the number of cases exploded, we issued a call to all available New York State-licensed nurses to help. Several days later, we expanded the call to include physician assistants. In the first week we received responses from one hundred twenty-two volunteers—ninety nurses, twelve doctors, and twenty others.

Quickly, it became apparent that the immense demands on first responders' time, coupled with the closing of schools, would create major childcare issues. For our first responders to be able to focus on their work, they needed to know that their children were secure. To solve the problem, we partnered with the state and school districts in Westchester to open their doors to the children of healthcare workers and first responders.

We also undertook an effort to reduce stress on local healthcare workers by teaming up with the Westchester Hotel Association and Westchester County Tourism & Film, to match guest-room donations to local hospitals for use by critical staff. Not only did this allow those workers to lessen their commutes between long shifts, but it also helped reduce possible exposure for their families.

In the first month of the pandemic, as we began to more

fully understand the nature of COVID-19, it became clear that securing a supply of personal protective equipment—masks, gloves, gowns, and face shields—on a massive scale was vitally important to slowing the spread of the virus. With PPE supplies increasingly hard to come by, we initiated a call for donations and set up a dedicated email address for persons interested in donating or selling us PPE. Over the following weeks, donations poured in. The American Chinese United Care Alliance gave PPE to our frontline workers, and major donations of masks for personal use came from Hanes Brands Inc. and the Greater New York Automobile Dealers Association. The masks were distributed to villages and towns and religious communities. And these donations, along with monetary gifts to Westchester Medical Center and White Plains Hospital, were a major boost in our fight against COVID-19.

Providing tax relief to our residents was crucial to mitigating the financial impact of the pandemic. We had no shortage of families suffering through furloughs and layoffs and struggling to put food on the table. We introduced legislation amending the Westchester County Tax Law to authorize towns to waive penalties for the late payment of county taxes until July 15. The governor authorized the plan, which gave our residents an additional seventy-six days to pay.

At the time of this writing—mid-January 2021—the vaccine has arrived, and we can see the beginning of the end. Of course, we still have a way to go, and the nearly eighteen hundred residents we lost during this cruel pandemic are never far from our thoughts.

Again, I think back to my parents' stories of the Great Depression and World War II, and I am convinced, with all of my heart, that we held up our end of the American bargain—to do the best we could to fight this virus and take care of our community.

Part 2

The Political and Public Policy Response to COVID-19

Part 3

The Political and Public Policy Response to COVID-19

20

Lessons Learned from COVID-19—A National Overview

By Matt Chase, Executive Director of the
National Association of Counties (NACo)

From the beginning, county officials and employees have worked tirelessly on the front lines of the COVID-19 pandemic, in communities large and small, to preserve both the lives of our residents and our way of life.

Starting with the Great Recession, the number of county and city public health jobs decreased by more than a quarter between 2008 and 2020, losing more than twenty-five thousand positions in one thousand nine hundred forty-three local government public health agencies. Large public health departments saw nearly a one-third drop in their budgets over that time, and small county health departments experienced about a 10 percent decrease.

This loss of funding has forced public health departments to shift their approach, reacting rather than anticipating threats and planning for them.

As a nation, we fund our health responses on a crisis-by-crisis basis—for H1N1 or Zika or Ebola or HIV/AIDS or opioids. This shortsighted pattern starved our public health functions. Thus, when a global pandemic like COVID-19 hits, it is no surprise the country isn't prepared. In fact, we were so unprepared that nine months after COVID-19 was detected here, there would only be two sparsely populated rural counties that did not register positive test results.

Sounding the Alarm

NACo started tracking the coronavirus early in 2020. San Diego County, California, was the first to take action, on February 14, when it declared a public health emergency so it could access state and federal funds to combat the spread of the virus. At the time, San Diego County was taking in U.S. overseas military personnel and family members from China, and the concern was that many of those individuals could be carrying COVID-19.

That was happening as NACo was adjusting the agenda for our 2020 Legislative Conference in Washington, D.C. We changed our programming and media tour to stress the danger posed by the virus. At a time when the national media was focused mainly on China, Europe, Washington state, California, and New York, it was essential to put counties across the nation on alert because we believed the virus would soon be moving inland from the coasts.

Dr. Robert Redfield, director of the Centers for Disease Control and Prevention, and CDC Chief Medical Officer Mitch Wolfe spoke to county officials, along with President Trump, at the NACo conference. Afterward, attendees headed home, and within a week were starting to take protective measures to slow the spread of the virus.

This was going to test counties in new, dramatic ways. Of course, preserving the lives and health of residents took precedence. Yet it was apparent that the economic consequences of life-saving measures would strain county budgets and reduce basic services. Counties were already funding human services to the tune of $58 billion annually before the pandemic, but soon we would be stacking responsibilities higher on a narrower tax base.

Financial Stability

As counties worked to save as many lives as possible, the federal and state governments worked to provide us with the resources we needed to accomplish the job.

Early on, Congress and the White House worked well together to pass a series of stimulus bills to help stabilize the economy. Congress also appropriated $500 billion for the U.S. Treasury and the Federal Reserve to create the Municipal Lending Facility (MLF), giving state and local governments access to credit when other financing routes were blocked by the chaos in traditional financial markets.

The MLF served as a backstop lender for the municipal bond market, which funds up to 80 percent of the nation's public infrastructure. That was a necessary move because investors had pulled $41 billion from that market in just a few days. Before the MLF was established, borrowing costs for local governments increased by up to 2.25 percent, and anyone who had a variable interest rate on their municipal bonds was facing dramatic increases.

The MLF and the financing opportunities it allowed for counties with populations of more than five hundred thousand was one of the most important actions the federal government took. It restored the confidence of the private markets that state and local governments and special purpose districts are still a sound investment. That not only was a lifeline to county governments, but it also calmed a jittery bond market.

A Little Help Here

That's not to overlook the impact of the overall Coronavirus Aid, Relief and Economic Security Act—the CARES Act. The $2.2 trillion stimulus package included the $150 billion Coronavirus Relief Fund, which supplied local governments with additional resources to pay for costs associated with fighting the pandemic. With direct payments to large counties and optional suballocations to smaller counties through state governments, counties had funding to purchase personal protective equipment, pay for social distancing measures to be installed in county facilities, and allow counties to make their own decisions about how to support our communities.

As general understanding increased around the nature of the virus's contagion, counties worked to secure non congregate housing not just for residents who needed a safe place to quarantine, but also shelter for unhoused residents who would otherwise be living in close quarters.

With extended closures to nonessential businesses adding up, counties provided services to out-of-work residents. Rental and utility assistance kept people in their homes, grants to small businesses kept the lights on, and local versions of the Paycheck Protection Program allowed businesses to pay their workers. Counties also lent a hand to the municipalities within their borders.

Some counties planned relief fund distributions with the impact of the virus in mind, directing funds to women- and minority-owned small businesses. Counties provided relief for struggling families with food procurement programs and also funded existing food banks.

As people stayed home, economic challenges, isolation, and psychological strains mounted. Counties saw increased demands on mental health, substance abuse, and domestic violence programs. Social service practitioners developed new service delivery strategies to work around physical distancing.

And with workers and students alike trying to work and study from home, many found that their internet connectivity couldn't handle the load. Counties set up broadband hotspots to expand access to high-speed internet.

As the playing field changed, the Coronavirus Relief Fund supported contact tracing costs as counties tried to get a handle on the extent of the virus's spread and provided hazard pay for county employees whose work put them in contact with the virus.

There were a few drawbacks to the CARES Act. The relief fund forbade counties from using the money to replace lost revenue. And counties with populations below five hundred thousand were at the mercy of state suballocation. Counties had a December 30 deadline to spend allocations, while at the same time, the pandemic had no respect for deadlines. This deadline was changed by Congress late in 2020, giving counties until the end of 2021 to spend CARES Act funds.

As late May approached, the federal response broke down along partisan lines. The Senate Republicans took a wait-and-see approach, thinking the pandemic would be short-lived. The House Democrats figured the pandemic would continue into 2021 and pushed for an additional relief package. Initially, the Trump administration sided with Senate Republicans, but as the pandemic continued, President Trump's negotiating position was closer to the House Democrats.

Senate Republicans represented states that were largely spared from the first two waves of the pandemic. Even their counties had a different experience based on their sources of local tax revenue. Counties that rely on property taxes didn't see the same impacts as those that rely on sales taxes and user fees to fund operations, such as New York counties.

Even within county governments, the effects of the pandemic varied when the courts, the clerks, and recorders—those functions that rely on user fees—saw them plummet to almost zero in March, April, and May. In many instances, the problem continues.

The Consequences of a Divided Nation

The federal government was a good banker for America's counties, but its role as a supplier needed a few attempts to adjust to the demands of the pandemic.

That was illustrated by the initial choice of the U.S. Department of Health and Human Services to distribute medical equipment. But PPE was a job better left to the Federal Emergency Management Agency, and the changeover in May was an improvement.

FEMA is accustomed to swift massive responses and brings connections with local emergency managers. While the response by the federal government has been uneven, there's been no lack of communication among federal partners.

Treating the pandemic as a disaster worthy of FEMA was apt. The nearly one quarter of all counties that have dealt with an event that rose to the level of a presidential disaster declaration were ready to react, falling back on previous plans and drawing on previous relationships built during action or in preparation. Practice doesn't always make perfect, but it cuts down on mistakes and, in this case, saved lives.

Part of the pain of the pandemic has come from facing the atrophy in our system of federalism. While we have seen disasters play out on local and regional levels, it has been a long time since a multistate emergency had federal, state, and local officials scrambling to find out who was in charge of what. Understandably, the regions that had practice and knew how to organize and communicate were better positioned to confront the virus.

If there's anything to be learned from the federal response, it's that we need a national strategy, including international collaboration. In the absence of one, states took their own approaches to combating the pandemic, which turned into a roller coaster ride.

Not having a comprehensive testing or contact tracing plan left counties with incomplete pictures of how the virus had spread in their communities. The long incubation period of COVID-19 and the number of asymptomatic carriers were already making the challenge harder, but unreliable and incomplete information added magnitudes of difficulty.

Another consequence of the fragmented response left counties, cities, and states bidding against each other for limited supplies of PPE, sometimes negotiating with dubious suppliers at inflated rates.

The lack of a national strategy was also reflected in the divisions that formed as the stress from the pandemic continued. The virus started on the coasts and moved inward at an uneven pace. As hotspots developed in certain regions, provincialism kicked in and the delineations followed: "That's a blue state problem" or "that's an urban problem." Soon enough, by the summer, the spikes were moving through the Sun Belt, and as November began, it was in the heartland.

That "us versus them" mentality is a national weakness and creates a false sense of security for those folks who weren't caught in the first phase or hotspots. The virus doesn't respect jurisdictional boundaries, and even nine months in, we were seeing a third spike in infections as winter came and people spent more time indoors.

We're still hoping to develop a national testing strategy, along with contact tracing, so we can reopen the economy. We know that testing and vaccines will not make the virus disappear, but they will allow us to interact with more confidence than we have now. These lessons learned should inform and improve our national strategy and rollout of vaccines and treatments for future pandemics.

The County Official

Even in the best of times, with record low unemployment and impressive national GDP growth, counties were still facing headwinds. There are a host of issues that are challenging; if you add a global pandemic on top of that, along with social unrest and a contentious election, local officials get caught in a perfect storm.

You can have legitimate policy arguments around our response, but we should all have shared values that the role of government is to protect and serve our residents. We can achieve this in a way that still protects our civil liberties.

We wish we didn't have to mandate masks. We wish that people would behave responsibly.

By no means are county officials perfect, but they have nowhere to hide from constituents. They grew up and live in the communities they serve. They're not picking up their briefcase and flying off to a distant location. At their best, they have the mindset that "we can succeed if we have a shared vision and remember that all of us are in this together." They're always around to hear residents' needs, complaints, and suggestions. Without question, they are our most responsive level of government.

Even so, it's hard for local elected officials to find a balance that pleases everyone while struggling to decide whether to try to keep people or the economy alive. Those are lose-lose situations. Often, those tensions boil over, like a customer slapping the hand of a Texas county judge who offered him a face mask in a store. It's the county official's job to remain calm and project that calm to constituents.

We have been siding with protecting life and looking at how we can safeguard people while restoring our economy. You can always bring back an economy, but the heartbreak of losing loved ones lingers forever.

And if the pandemic wasn't enough, county leaders are still responsible for maintaining infrastructure, working with elections administrators, managing criminal justice reform, and more. The world doesn't stop because of COVID-19.

Where counties excelled was their focus on problem solving. How can we help people in need? How can we figure out how best to deliver scarce resources? This mentality has delivered unprecedented levels of collaboration with chambers of commerce and learning how to help small businesses and manufacturers. Counties are using the bulk of federal aid not to fund our own operations, but to inject resources into our communities. We're seeing counties help the smallest of the small businesses and the nonprofit sector in an even greater way than before the pandemic. The comeback won't be easy, but it would have been far harder without the partnerships developed over the last nine months.

We saw some wins for counties start to bear fruit. As e-commerce exploded with residents staying home, the Marketplace Fairness Act brought tax revenue to rural communities that aren't traditional shopping centers.

We should never be complacent, and that's the role of public-sector leaders, dispensing optimism about our future and preparing us for the darker hours—some of them predictable, others that will catch us off guard.

COVID-19 taught county leaders three important lessons. The first: Long-term planning matters. This means practicing for a disaster, knowing who you need to talk to and who your partners can be. The second: Saving funds during the best of times to prepare for the worst of times is crucial. The costs to fix something that has been turned upside down are astronomical. The third: We've learned that there is no such thing as a status quo, and we need to be ready whether it's a global pandemic and waves of unemployment, terrorist attack, or a natural disaster. Getting ready to fight a future emergency is hard and expensive work. But it leads us to the most important question of all: Can a great nation that wants to remain great afford to do any less?

21

A Federal(ist) Response to the Public Health Crisis

The American system of government is complicated. It has a national government, of course, the state governments, and over twenty thousand local governments. Counties and other local governments are the backbone of our communities providing our residents with needed services.

Despite the reliance on government services being fulfilled by county government, the U.S. Constitution does not include any reference to local governments. The federal government almost always works directly through the states and not directly with the local governments, with few exceptions, and it is the states, through their own constitutions and laws, that pass these federal requirements to the counties.

During this pandemic, Vice President Mike Pence, chair of the White House Coronavirus Task Force, said the country's COVID-19 response was federally supported, state managed, and locally executed. That would have been ideal. But a lack of a consistent national strategy forced states to take their own approaches, often leaving local government leaders, and the public, to figure out who was in charge of what.

Testing Federalism

To understand some of that confusion about who was in charge, one need only to look at our nation's historic federalism debate. Our founding fathers struggled with the concept of whether a federal government or the states should hold more power in our nation. Alexander Hamilton, James Madison, and John Jay were proponents of a stronger, more centralized federal government as the chief authors of the Federalist Papers, while Thomas Jefferson led the charge in favor of a more decentralized form of government.

In the late 1700s, Hamilton and those who believed that there should be a strong centralized government won out. The power of the purse, a centralized monetary system with the ability to borrow at the federal level, helped fund the Revolutionary War, as well as every war after that. Today, only the federal government can engage in deficit spending, not the states and not local governments. That is how Congress was able to pass the stimulus packages.

However, even with a structure that provides federal government broad powers, our system still protects many rights and responsibilities of state and local governments.

This is a strength that allows for diverse policies and flexibility in ways to respond to emergencies. But the strength of our system can also be a weakness or confusing to citizens when an issue strikes that could arguably best be handled by all levels of government rowing in the same direction.

At times we saw this weakness exposed with the COVID-19 pandemic battle. The pandemic tested federalism, as leaders debated which level of government should manage different aspects of the response. There were parts of the federal government that had obvious responsibilities: the Food and Drug Administration (FDA), the Centers for Disease Control and Prevention, and the Department of Health and Human Services, and the Federal Emergency Management Agency. Congress, as well, played its role in allocating funding to many of the areas of our society most impacted by the pandemic. But the pandemic impacted states in different ways, causing the federal government to sometimes act inconsistently, creating confusion as to whether it was centralizing the response or leaving that up to governors and their administrations.

Interestingly, the federalist, power-sharing structure was also tested at the state level. While the president handed the response to the states, in New York, Governor Andrew Cuomo used extraordinary, emergency executive powers to centralize the response rather than relying on counties, which had the statutory responsibility to respond to public health emergencies. Other states followed the president's philosophy and let counties and local governments determine local response policies. This patchwork of power made it more difficult both at a national level and for states, local government leaders, and residents to know who was in charge, which government officials to listen to, and which edicts to follow.

A Wedge Further Divides the Nation

It wasn't just federalism that caused power vacuums. Party politics was also at play in the federal government's pandemic response.

It was a presidential election year. Control of both houses of Congress was at stake in the election. Perhaps that should not matter during a national emergency. But it did matter more this year because the country was more politically divided than it had been in recent history, with Democrats and Republicans at odds over just about every major issue.

The Democratic-led House of Representatives had just voted to impeach the president, but the Republican-led Senate voted against conviction. In addition to the trial, the Senate confirmed the appointment of a new Supreme Court justice, and both the timing and the pick seemed to increase the political divisions. Meanwhile, the Democratic Party was holding presidential primaries to choose a candidate to run against President Trump, who made controversial and often divisive statements about the candidates and other high-profile Democrats.

It was into this politically charged atmosphere that the

coronavirus arrived. For county leaders in New York State, politics was a distant second to the need for support from the federal government to respond to the public health emergency. County officials—Republicans and Democrats—worked together to respond to the pandemic, and together they urged their representatives in Congress to do the same. However, nationally, Republicans and Democrats could not agree on a bill to help states and local governments.

Congress Funds PPE and PPP, but not New York's Counties

At the beginning of March, dozens of New York county officials joined thousands of county leaders from across the nation in Washington for NACo's annual Legislative Conference. As usual, the local leaders split time between attending conference events and meeting with their state's congressional delegation. But this year was different.

As they landed at Ronald Reagan Airport that Sunday, Wolf Blitzer was on CNN talking about this new virus that had found its way to the United States in a nursing home in the state of Washington and then to California. Over the next two days, the county officials met with nine members of the New York congressional delegation, representatives from the White House, and the state's U.S. senators, Senate Minority Leader Charles Schumer and Senator Kirsten Gillibrand. The sense of caution that hung in the air heightened with every meeting over the three days. Their last meeting was with Senator Gillibrand, who had just received a somber briefing from the vice president on the novel coronavirus epidemic that was spreading across the country.

Throughout the pandemic, county leaders lobbied their federal representatives for funding for counties, particularly as Congress considered a series of coronavirus relief measures. New York counties were in a particular bind because they were on the front lines of the pandemic at the same time state officials were threatening to make them pay more for the state's Medicaid program, which was already costing county taxpayers $7.5 billion in local funds every year. Early county lobbying efforts paid off. Later efforts were not as successful.

On March 14, Congress passed the Families First Coronavirus Response Act (H.R. 6201), which provided federal paid sick leave, food assistance funding, and most important for counties, an increase in the percentage of Medicaid funding that the federal government would give New York State and its counties. The bill enhanced the Federal Medicaid Assistance Percentage (eFMAP) from 50 percent to 56.2 percent for the federal share. That was a lifeline of between $5 and $7 billion for New York State.

This was a big win for New York State and its counties. The reason for federal enhancement for FMAP is that the federal government is willing to support additional costs for states during a national crisis to prevent state funding cuts in key health programs. This has been the federal policy since the Great Recession.

For counties in New York, which contribute to the state's

share of Medicaid costs, the savings was $160 million per quarter. This included $95 million in savings for New York City and $65 million for the rest of the counties in the state. By the end of 2020, counties had saved $495 million. There will be another $160 million in savings for each quarter the federal emergency declaration lasts. The Biden administration has indicated it is likely to keep the emergency in place through the end of 2021, which could generate additional county and New York City savings of $640 million. Looking back, the actions that Congress took through the pandemic focused on: providing cash to individuals to offset income losses or spur economic activity; an increase in unemployment benefits to support those who lost their jobs; the Paycheck Protection Program designed to help small (and some larger) businesses pay employees, rent, and utilities; aid to schools and colleges; funding for personal protection equipment; and a boost in federal Medicaid funding. What the 116th Congress didn't provide was direct and flexible funding that the State of New York and its counties wanted to help offset revenue losses and the costs of responding to the emergency. Fortunately, that help would come a year later from the next Congress.

The third bill Congress passed was the Coronavirus Aid, Relief, and Economic Securities Act (CARES Act) (H.R. 748), which was signed into law on March 27, 2020. It was the largest COVID-19 stimulus package, providing a federal appropriation close to $3 trillion. This legislation included the creation of a $150 billion Coronavirus Relief Fund, supplying large communities, including counties with a population greater than five hundred thousand, with federal relief to aid in COVID-19 response efforts. This legislation also extended the expiration of the federal Temporary Assistance for Needy Families program (TANF), $45 billion for FEMA's Disaster Relief Fund, $400 million in election assistance, an additional $600 a week in federal funding for unemployment assistance, and $377 billion for the Paycheck Protection Program to help small business through the economic shutdown without laying off their employees.

Despite calls for another stimulus bill, the Senate and House of Representatives could not agree on another stimulus approach through most of the rest of the year. Congress did not take up another compromise bill until December 23. And that bill, once approved, did not get signed by the president until December 26, the day after Christmas and the week that enhanced unemployment benefits were set to expire.

Throughout the spring, summer, and fall, NYSAC and county leaders had lobbied their federal representatives to pass a stimulus bill that would provide funding for states and local governments that were most impacted by COVID-19. They sought direct funding support from the federal government to help them deliver an array of social services, including public assistance, heating assistance, child support, and adult programs.

The problem for New York's counties was that they were delivering these programs at a time when the state was cutting local assistance to close a state budget deficit that grew from $6 billion before the pandemic to nearly $15 billion as income and sales tax revenue plummeted with the economic shutdown. The state, then, was cutting aid to counties and other local governments. Recognizing that they were not going to get help from the state, counties turned to their congressional members to plead for support.

New York's county leaders continued to advocate for unrestricted, direct aid for states, counties, and other local governments throughout the summer and fall, including during a tense set of negotiations between Speaker of the House Nancy Pelosi and Secretary of the Treasury Steve Mnuchin. NYSAC and the counties of New York were on the phone nonstop with the Speaker Pelosi's office and Senate Minority Leader Chuck Schumer trying to hammer out a deal. After months of negotiation, thousands of lives and livelihoods lost, and the emergence of a full-blown second wave, Congress finally struck a deal on a nearly $900 billion COVID-19 relief package just days before Christmas, but it left counties out in the cold. While the agreement provided relief to families and businesses, it did not provide direct, unrestricted aid to counties and the state.

This failure of federal government to come to the aid of states and local governments in a time of national emergency was unprecedented and placed local governments in the direct line of a triple economic threat: loss of $1.2 billion in local sales tax revenue; $600 million in state reimbursement cuts; and an increased demand for social services like home heating, food stamps, and meals on wheels.

The White House's Way

Early in January, Health and Human Services Secretary Alex Azar was made aware of a novel coronavirus spreading through a seafood market in the Wuhan Province in China. Chinese authorities refused Azar's offer to send a team from the Centers for Disease Control and Prevention, and this lack of cooperation from China put the rest of the world at a significant disadvantage when cases began to spread around the globe.

When the first cases of COVID-19 were found in the state of Washington and California, then in New York, counties looked to the federal government for leadership and direction. Advice started to come from the White House Coronavirus Task Force, which suggested the novel coronavirus was three times more infectious than the flu, and the risk of serious illness was highest for seniors and those with compromised immune systems. They warned that long-term care facilities, like nursing homes, were at the highest risk.

On March 3, President Trump addressed thousands of county officials at the National Association of Counties Conference. He lauded county health departments for their work responding to coronavirus contagion.

> "Six weeks ago, eight weeks ago, you never heard of this. All of a sudden it's got the world aflutter. Things happen that you never even think would happen and you have to confront it, you have to do a lot of good work and you

> take care of the situation. You people do it better than anyone I can think of. America has the world's most advanced public health system. We know that our county health officials play a front-line role in battling public health threats and we are working with Congress very closely to pass supplemental legislation to ensure state and county health departments get everything they need."

On March 13, the president declared a national emergency and announced the start of a fifteen-day Slow the Spread campaign designed by the CDC to help stop the pandemic in the United States. The campaign recommended that Americans listen to state and local authorities, stay home if they feel sick, and quarantine if a family member tests positive for COVID-19. The Slow the Spread campaign was extended through April.

By March 20, the federal government was focused on testing and providing therapies to treat COVID-19. The president signed legislation to ensure Americans were tested for free, streamlined the reporting of test results, and appointed Admiral Brett Giroir, the assistant secretary of health at HHS,, to coordinate coronavirus testing efforts. The FDA issued emergency approval for new commercial coronavirus tests and began allowing states to authorize tests developed and used by their own laboratories. The FDA also started exploring new and existing drugs that could be used to treat COVID-19.

By April 2, President Trump was pondering domestic travel restrictions, possibly to and from hotspots via air, rail, or other travel and said that some kind of face covering, masks or a scarf when out in public was not a bad idea, but there was still no formal recommendation.

Governor Cuomo held daily televised briefings designed at first to talk to New Yorkers about the status of the pandemic, but his audience quickly grew beyond the borders of New York. Many of these briefings had a federal component, where the governor discussed the requests he made to the president and the federal government, particularly for supplies of PPE and ventilators, and more hospital beds.

Responding to the Needs of New York

As leader of the National Governors Association, Cuomo was part of the regular calls between the president and governors from across the nation. He would often reference these calls during his daily briefing. Sometimes he would applaud President Trump for his handling of the virus, but just as often, he would criticize him. In the end, though, most of Governor Cuomo's requests were met by the federal government, and the governor acknowledged them when aid was provided.

On March 28, at the request of Governor Cuomo, the president sent the *USS Comfort*, a Navy hospital ship with one thousand beds, to New York Harbor to supplement the existing number of beds. The ship arrived on March 30. In addition, FEMA and HHS helped build temporary hospital sites in New York City, on Long Island, and in Westchester County, including a six hundred-bed nursing home facility in Brooklyn. These were the hardest-hit areas of the state, and they were the first major targets of support from the state and federal governments. This was a breathtaking example of how the federal government could mobilize resources in a short period of time.

At this point in the pandemic, hospitals, states, and counties were having trouble acquiring PPE supplies to protect their front-line emergency responders and healthcare workers. Through FEMA, HHS, and the Defense Department, the federal government started distributing supplies of PPE and ventilators from the Strategic National Stockpile.

At the prodding of Governor Cuomo, the president issued an executive order invoking the Defense Production Act. Under this law, the president has the authority to ask the country's manufacturers to make and distribute the health and medical supplies in a national emergency. This first order required General Motors to shift some of their manufacturing capacity to make ventilators. Later, the administration expanded this Defense Production Act order to include General Electric and other companies to make ventilators and 3M to make PPE.

It was becoming clear that the pandemic was inequitably impacting communities of color, raising red flags for local public health officials. Dr. Anthony Fauci explained that the likely reason for this was that members of these communities were more likely to have pre-existing conditions that predispose them to greater impact from COVID-19, and many individuals in these communities lacked access to routine medical care.

The federal government at this time recognized the impact the virus was having in New York State while other states seemed to be avoiding the sharp increase that New York experienced.

Transitioning to a New President, New Congress, and New Plan of Attack

President Joseph R. Biden, Jr. was inaugurated on January 20, 2021, taking office during the second wave of infections as the vaccines were being sent to states, and there were calls from state and local governments for another federal stimulus package. Among Biden's first acts as president was signing an order that required masks be worn on all federally owned lands and parks, and he pledged to purchase an additional one hundred million doses of vaccines from the two manufacturers that had approved vaccines on the market since December.

The Senate, now comprised of fifty Democrats and fifty Republicans, shifted its majority because Democrat Vice President Kamala Harris had the deciding vote. Senator Charles Schumer became the first Senate majority leader from New York. Democrats also held a slim majority in the House of Representatives. With majorities in both houses of Congress, President Biden was able to advance a new

$1.9 billion federal stimulus package designed to help bring an end to the pandemic and foster an economic rebound. Majority Leader Schumer worked with the Speaker Pelosi to ensure there was nearly $350 billion in the stimulus package for states and local governments to help offset lost revenue and the cost of fighting the pandemic, and to help rebuild local economies.

The President pledged to work with Democrats and Republicans to defeat the pandemic and revive the economy, support the educational system, and restore a common sense of purpose that had been shaken by the global health crisis and brutal divisiveness that gripped the nation for the past several years.

22

Tilting the Power Structure in New York

New York has a history of local government authority dating back to the 1600s. Some of New York's counties were formed during the Colonial era. Today, there are 1,607 local governments, with 62 counties, 62 cities, 932 towns, and 551 villages. The State Constitution provides for the structure, powers, and operational procedures of these local governments, and the Local Government Bill of Rights is codified in the state's Home Rule Law.

Under the Constitution's Home Rule provisions, local legislative bodies are granted broad powers to adopt local laws in order to carry out their governmental responsibilities. These powers are among the most far-reaching in the country.

Historically, the extent of these powers has made local governments in New York almost equal partners with the state in the shared responsibility for providing services to the people. This partnership was tested by the powers assumed by Governor Cuomo during the pandemic.

Expanding State Executive Powers

The language was simple. The ramifications were more complicated.

During the late hours of Monday, March 2, more than two weeks before the COVID-19 pandemic was declared, the State Legislature passed Governor Program Bill 8. This legislation also provided for a $40 million public health emergency appropriation for the governor to fight the pandemic. The bill's language gave Governor Cuomo unprecedented powers in an unprecedented time, the largest and most aggressive global public health crisis in more than 100 years. These powers allowed him to make laws without a vote of state lawmakers.

In fact, the State Legislature shaped how the governor could use these executive powers to fight the pandemic by expanding his powers and making it clear that under law a virus such as COVID-19 could qualify as a statewide emergency. New York Executive Law, Section 29a was changed to now read (in relevant parts with changes in brackets and underlined):

> Subject to the state constitution, the federal constitution and federal statutes and regulations, the governor may by executive order temporarily suspend [~~specific provisions~~

> ~~of~~] any statute, local law, ordinance, or orders, rules or regulations, or parts thereof, of any agency during a state disaster emergency, if compliance with such provisions would prevent, hinder, or delay action necessary to cope with the disaster or if necessary to assist or aid in coping with such disaster. The governor, by executive order, may issue any directive during a state disaster emergency declared in the following instances: fire, flood, earthquake, hurricane, tornado, high water, landslide, mudslide, wind, storm, wave action, volcanic activity, epidemic, disease outbreak, air contamination, terrorism, cyber event, blight, drought, infestation, explosion, radiological accident, nuclear, chemical, biological, or bacteriological release, water contamination, bridge failure or bridge collapse. Any such directive must be necessary to cope with the disaster and may provide for procedures reasonably necessary to enforce such directive.

The clear inclusion of "epidemic" and "disease outbreak" as emergencies that would qualify under these expanded gubernatorial powers helped keep future challenges to this authority at bay. There is little case law that defines the extent of the reach of executive orders (EO) in the declaration of a statewide emergency, which is more commonly used for natural disasters such as high-level floods, hurricanes, ice storms, or superstorms like Irene, which slammed New York State just over a decade ago. The unprecedented redistribution of power, included as part of the state's coronavirus response efforts, gave the governor these emergency powers for more than a year, until April 1, 2021. The powers were revoked in an act signed by the Legislature, which was signed by the governor on March 7, 2021.

This section of law, in its previous version, was invoked by Governor George E. Pataki in 2001, after the terrorist attack on New York City on 9/11. Rarely has this declaration been invoked for a public health-related emergency such as a virus, with a notable exception of 2018, when Governor Cuomo declared an emergency to battle the spiking levels of the flu. At that time, he used it to sign an executive order to allow pharmacists to give the flu vaccine to children. The pandemic as an emergency on a far greater scale, and this scale was reflected in the breadth of the powers the governor quickly began to exercise.

Five days after the State Legislature granted him these extraordinary powers, on March 7, 2020, he signed his first COVID-19 Executive Order 202, declaring "a State disaster emergency for the entire State of New York. This Executive Order shall be in effect until September 7, 2020."

In addition to expanding the governor's executive powers, the State Legislature also ceded substantial fiscal powers to the governor in the adoption of the state fiscal year (SFY) 2020-21 State Budget. The enacted budget granted significant powers to the budget director, who works directly for the governor, to maintain a balanced budget for the 2020–21 fiscal year. The budget gave authority and discretion to the budget director to withhold or reduce funding in the Aid to Localities Budget to respond to the direct and indirect economic, financial, and social effects of the COVID-19 pandemic.

These three actions—1. granting the governor expanded executive orders in emergency declarations, 2. the governor's first executive order, and 3. allowing the budget director to unilaterally cut Aid to Local Governments—greatly upended the power balance in the State Capitol. The traditional way of governing in New York State was set aside once Governor Cuomo declared the state of emergency. The executive branch became much more powerful than the legislative branch, and the state was set up to have much more power over local governments.

Ultimately, the governor enacted over one hundred executive orders (EOs) amending scores of state and local laws, rules and regulations to address the public health emergency. These EOs carry the same weight as any other law enacted by the State Legislature on a temporary basis during the state of emergency.

The EOs, many of them controversial and constitutionally questionable, directed how residents could live, work, and seek entertainment, practice religion, get food, access shelter, and move about in their communities. They addressed K-12 school operations and college schedules, deemed businesses essential or nonessential, and closed all in-person operations of nonessential businesses. The

EOs required new mandates on hospitals, nursing homes, healthcare practices, and local governments and regulated other aspects of society. Many of these directives had to be enforced by state and local government officials, mostly local, which also raised issues with some of the new limits on individual freedoms, which were historically protected by the constitutions of the state and federal governments.

Limiting the Power of Local Governments

Interestingly, some of the first executive orders were directed at counties to limit their authority to act during the state of emergency. The third EO, 202.3, declared that any local emergency order, or charter, law, or regulation, that is in conflict with a New York State executive order is suspended. The governor essentially took control of governing New Yorkers through the pandemic, limiting the power of local leaders and requiring local governments to simply enforce the state's directives. That was his prerogative under the authority given to him by the Legislature.

By direction of the governor, the counties' long-established emergency management protocol and home-rule authority were set aside in favor of a uniform state response. While the state needed county governments to provide services and enforcement, it was quickly understood that the governor would lean on a new centralized statewide command system and not allow local governments to pursue a regional approach.

Executive Order 202.4, required local governments

and counties to reduce their on-site workforce, directing at least 50 percent of all nonessential personnel work from home. This was arguably an unconstitutional act, as the property and affairs of government were reserved for the local governments by the State Constitution and immune from state interference. Nonetheless, the EO exempted personnel who were "essential" to responding to the COVID-19 pandemic, and counties needed to determine which employees were essential and which weren't. The workforce reduction was intended to keep people from working too close together and make it easier for employees to keep socially distant. The term "essential" meant that they must perform their work on the job site, and not from home.

"When you start to look at who is essential in this fight, you really can't have anyone from the sheriff's office, or the county health department, or the department of public works work from home. They are all essential," said one county official at the March 17 county leaders' meeting. Later in the year, the State Legislature passed a law signed by the governor which required local governments to submit a list of essential and nonessential employees to the state.

The 50 percent workforce reduction numbers that were set forth in these first EOs were expanded a couple of days later, requiring 75 percent of the workforce to work from home. And then, a week later, new EOs required all nonessential employees to work from home. This required counties to determine which positions were essential and which were nonessential. Again, the process worked, and the legislation was unnecessary.

While many executive orders were designed primarily to slow or stop the spread of the virus, some tested the constitutional power of the state over local governments. One EO that tested the traditional balance of power was issued a week before Thanksgiving. It limited gatherings in private homes to no more than ten people. A number of county sheriffs quickly questioned the constitutionality of the EO and said they would not enforce it.

Erie County Sheriff Timothy B. Howard said, "This national holiday has created longstanding family traditions that are at the heart of America, and these traditions should not be stopped or interrupted by Governor Cuomo's mandates." He said he would not be enforcing the order.

Governor Cuomo responded: "I don't believe as a law enforcement officer, you have a right to pick and choose what laws you will enforce. That is frankly frightening to me as an individual, frightening to democracy. It's arrogant, and it violates your constitutional duty."

Fulton County Sheriff Richard Giardino, a well-respected former county judge, questioned the constitutionality of the order in the first place and said that was why his office would not be enforcing it. Several other sheriffs also announced they would not be checking whether family gatherings exceeded the ten-person limit, especially over the Thanksgiving holiday.

23

Unifying and Informing New York's Counties

In mid-March, government leaders, public health officials, and healthcare professionals at all levels were simply trying to understand this novel coronavirus when they put together a plan to stop it from spreading. An apt analogy used often during the pandemic was that government was assembling the airplane in the middle of the flight. The great challenge was that county leaders had to fly these planes with incomplete directions and sometimes conflicting information.

In a typical emergency event, local governments would declare a state of emergency if the conditions warranted it within their county. If it was broad, the state would declare such emergency. However, this was no typical emergency, and confusion commenced at the onset of the outbreak with a state of emergency declared in all fifty states.

That is when county leaders first turned to the New York State Association of Counties (NYSAC). The Association was well-attuned to the work of government at all levels and knew better than most others the role of New York's counties in this broader federal-state-local public policy context. NYSAC knew where and how to find the answers that county officials needed during this pandemic.

To help avoid confusion and provide information to county leaders, NYSAC needed a way to share this type of information with every county at the same time. That's when NYSAC started hosting daily conference calls with county leaders across the state. Later switching to Zoom, NYSAC held dozens of meetings with county leaders to clarify executive orders, provide feedback on state policies, and discuss the unvarnished county perspective of the pandemic at a time when most other information was incomplete, inaccurate, or filtered through a state or federal perspective.

County Leaders Meetings: Providing Updates During the Crisis

On March 12, NYSAC hosted a meeting of county leaders to update county officials on the second coronavirus stimulus package passed by Congress. The meeting included county executives, chairs of county legislative boards, and county administrators. The primary focus was the impact of the stimulus package on counties, but it also included a COVID-19 briefing by New York City Mayor Bill de Blasio, who detailed the public health response efforts in the city and what other county leaders could expect as the coronavirus spread across the state. "We all have to work to help each other because ultimately, we have the same goal in mind—saving lives," de Blasio told the county leaders.

This meeting became the model that NYSAC used to keep counties connected and bridge communication between the political, geographic, and demographic boundaries that often separated more densely populated and more liberal leaning downstate regions with the more rural and conservative upstate regions.

Since that first meeting, NYSAC convened leaders from across the state more than 50 times over the next twelve months, first in March, April, and May, and then restarting these meetings in December, January, and February when the second and third waves of COVID-19 infections swept across the state.

These leadership forums were part fireside chat and part information exchange on state executive orders and activities, mixed in with urgent action alerts on the state budget and additional federal stimulus negotiations. These meetings also became a platform through which the county leaders could trade ideas on securing PPE; brainstorm ways to shift internal resources and save money; and discuss how counties were managing the process of essential testing, contact tracing, and enforcing isolation and quarantine orders on residents who had been exposed to the virus.

The meetings were led and moderated by NYSAC Executive Director Stephen Acquario, who typically started with a motivational leadership anecdote designed to inspire and connect the county leaders to the crucial, public service responsibility at hand. The agenda then included: 1. new Association COVID-19 resources; 2. a COVID-19 update that included new positive cases and hospitalizations; 3. an update on new state executive orders and announcements by Governor Cuomo; 4. a discussion of federal activities; and 5. an opportunity for the county leaders to ask questions or make comments. Some meetings included a guest speaker that provided attendees with specific information or examples of best COVID-fighting practices. (See Appendix C for a sample county leaders meeting agenda.)

Meeting Demands for Personal Protective Equipment

Local governments are responsible for ensuring emergency responders have access to the personal protective equipment they need in a public health emergency. However, during the first several months of the pandemic, county leaders were having trouble getting the PPE these front-line workers needed, including N95 respirators, surgical and face masks, face shields, gowns, coveralls, and gloves—all designed to protect wearers from exposure to the air particles that spread the virus.

There were many instances of counties helping counties during the pandemic. They are too numerous to mention. But a few stories deserve to be highlighted.

Supplies were low and demand was high, not just for counties. Hospitals and nursing homes did not have the supply they needed to protect nurses, doctors and other staff who were caring for patients. While most PPE is designed for single use, nurses were reusing masks and turning gowns inside out for a second use.

Executive Director Acquario observed: "It was a scary thought that we could not protect those whose sole purpose is to protect others from the invisible enemy. We knew this was going to be a major problem if this early in the outbreak we could not properly protect the front-line healthcare workers and essential workers. And this was not just a local problem, it was a challenging problem to address globally."

The Strategic National Stockpile (SNS) had considerable storage of personal protective equipment, but not enough to meet demands. States were competing with and outbidding other states to buy PPE, and the pricing for these masks, gloves, and gowns was rising significantly.

Governor Cuomo addressed the shortage in one of his daily briefings, suggesting that it was overwhelming local government procurement and emergency management departments, so he wanted to centralize PPE acquisition and distribution. He said that if the federal government did not take over the purchase of PPE, then states would continue competing against each other, raising the price of the precious, life-saving commodity.

"He was right. New York was bidding against Illinois, California, and Florida," Executive Director Acquario said. "The same mask that cost 85 cents before the pandemic now cost $7. The governor desperately wanted federal intervention. He was right. It was an unfortunate and preventable mess."

The mess was made worse on March 28, when the governor announced that the state had received a large shipment of PPE and would centralize the supply and distribute it to counties based on need. Each county had to submit a plan for how they were managing their emergency operations centers. The State Office of Emergency Management (OEM) was supposed to contact each county OEM to find out what they needed for PPE. But for most counties, that supply was not provided by the state, whose priority was still focused on providing resources to the more populated and impacted downstate counties and New York City.

Without federal coordination and a lack of adequate supplies coming from the state, upstate rural counties and towns scrambled to figure out how to acquire PPE for their nursing homes and EMS, public safety, and healthcare workers. It was a state-against-state scramble, but also a state-versus-local government scramble.

County leaders began to share their local PPE needs at NYSAC's county leaders' meetings and in emails to the Association. Dutchess County, under the leadership of County Executive Marcus Molinaro, had sufficient PPE and indicated that it could help others based on need. And when Dutchess needed supplies, other counties would help Dutchess in return. It was the pinnacle of shared services, local governments working together in their finest hour. NYSAC's executive director acted as the conduit for the need and personally drove the supplies from one region of the state to other regions.

In his first PPE expedition, Executive Director Acquario

picked up boxes of supplies in Dutchess County and brought them to the Herkimer County in the Mohawk Valley, where deputy sheriffs from a dozen counties convened to secure their allotment. County officials drove hundreds of miles, some as far as Chautauqua County, the furthest western-border county in New York. County Executive Molinaro personally loaded the boxes himself wishing all in need "Godspeed."

The governor's office was concerned with the counties' exchanges of personal protective equipment, and a state representative questioned Stephen Acquario. "They wanted to know what we were doing," he said, "so I told them it was the job of local emergency managers to provide PPE to first responders and healthcare workers in their communities, especially if they cannot secure them from the state or federal governments or on their own. The state representative said county governments would get what they needed, not what they wanted."

The state's calculations took into account the use and reuse of masks by nurses in a healthcare setting. The state had the number of nurses in each county and distributed PPE based on these numbers.

"I had to explain that nursing homes, first responders, and EMS needed more," Stephen Acquario said. "Hospitals were reporting they needed more, and nurses disagreed with the number of times the mask should be reused. The counties were helping each other and the front-line healthcare workers who in turn helped others in the public. The state's position was that it was in charge of PPE, not the counties, and if the counties wanted more, they needed to request them from the state. I recall thinking the last thing we needed was a divisive partnership with the state, especially now. We needed to work together and not compete against one another. Lives were at stake." In his next transport, after surveying the needs of the North Country, Executive Director Acquario brought supplies again from Dutchess County to the Warren County Municipal Center where deputy sheriffs, county administrators, and public health staff from across the vast and rural six-million-acre rural North Country region convened to pick up their allotment of donated PPE.

"It was all very random. The 'SOS call' would go out at any hour, and counties responded. If a county had PPE that could be spared, they lent it to another county in desperate need. It was a breathtaking act of humanity each time the PPE was shared, as it could be potentially life-saving. And it was always reciprocal. As the virus ebbed and flowed so did the demand for PPE. Gowns, gloves, surgical masks, face shields were the most in demand. It was like a mobile army surgical supply operation. It was work till you drop government, 15-hour days, seven days a week for 150 days," said the NYSAC Executive Director.

Sharing Testing Kits

It wasn't just PPE that the counties shared. Nurses, test kits, and even body bags were in short supply in some counties throughout the pandemic. And when there was a need for assistance, the counties that could stepped up to help.

When COVID-19 was spreading rapidly in its nursing homes, Steuben County received little guidance or resources from the state. Again, NYSAC's executive director sent out a call for help. He brought tests and gowns donated from Dutchess, Albany, and Onondaga counties to the rural county in the Finger Lakes Region. Here's an excerpt of a letter sent by Steuben County Administrator Jack Wheeler in late 2020 to NYSAC President Jack Marren to recognize NYSAC's efforts.

> "In early April, Steuben County experienced a massive outbreak of the virus in three nursing homes simultaneously. We pressed NYSDOH to help support us in universal testing of staff and residents in these facilities, with them placing the caveat that we had to provide the testing supplies. At the time, our county had less than one hundred PCR swabs on hand and required at least five hundred to complete those urgent tests… Steve… immediately hit the road to the Hudson Valley, back to Albany, and over to Syracuse to borrow swabs from other counties, along with some PPE for the testing events.
>
> "He met one of our sheriffs' deputies in Syracuse to hand off the supplies, and as a

> result, we were able to begin testing at the nursing homes the following day. Without his selflessness and creativity, I am sure we would have been delayed by a number of days, putting additional nursing home residents at jeopardy. I honestly believe his actions helped save lives of a vulnerable population in our county."

Early on in the public health crisis, when things were worse on Long Island than they were upstate, Onondaga County sent nurses to Suffolk County when it needed them. Another example of county leader stepping up to help was Albany County Executive Daniel McCoy's assistance to other counties. In the third week of May, at the request of Broome County, McCoy provided 1,000 COVID-19 test kits to Acquario, who in turn picked them up at the County Office Building and delivered them at 10 p.m. to a Broome County public safety officer to test nursing home residents. Broome officials frequently drove the 280 miles to deliver COVID test kits to the state lab in Albany to get results for their residents. It mattered that much to County Executive Jason Garnar to get the results as soon as possible, and this was the only way to get those results.

In its darkest hour, New York City Mayor Bill de Blasio stood shoulder to shoulder with upstate county leaders, offering to help with PPE and lab testing. The PPE supply purchasing power of the city was important, and NYSAC was in frequent contact with the mayor's office. The city had a plethora of talented public servants, and they frequently lent their expertise to counties throughout the state.

And later, in the fall of 2020, Livingston County put out a request for twenty-five body bags, which were backordered by their supplier. Again, using the system that was in place to help "triage" the local PPE needs, NYSAC Executive Director Acquario met up with a Livingston County sheriff's deputy on a Friday evening in Oneida County to transfer a supply of body bags. "The bags were heavy and extremely durable," he noted. "I had never seen a body bag before, and delivering them was a somber moment for me. I wondered who would be zipped up in them, and I felt for the pain that these families would have to endure."

Cooperative Purchase of PPE

During March and April, many upstate county leaders asked NYSAC to coordinate a multicounty purchase of PPE so that the counties could get a better price and ensure a steady supply. Dutchess County Commissioner of Emergency Response Dana Smith found a supplier with a Chinese PPE manufacturer, and he began to work with NYSAC to coordinate a limited joint purchase—limited because the amount of PPE that they could purchase would not be able to supply more than a dozen counties.

Stephen Acquario recalled: "We were connected to several 'PPE brokers' each claiming they did N95 mask procurement and all forms of PPE acquisition for hospitals in New York City. They said they could negotiate with the

Chinese manufacturers of the PPE. I asked Dana Smith to join these conversations. We surveyed the counties and created an Excel spread sheet detailing the type of PPE needed. We talked about purchasing two hundred to three hundred thousand. The price fluctuated daily. The broker promised us fifty thousand masks, and within minutes while on the phone, it was reduced to forty-nine thousand five hundred masks at $5.08 per N95 mask and eight-five cents per surgical mask."

Commissioner Smith's previous job was testing the fit of respirators. He would inspect and pick up the masks, which were supposed to be flown into Connecticut, not far from Dutchess County. The PPE would be distributed from there. But transaction details kept changing on the supplier end.

"We had orders from eleven counties, ranging from five hundred for Chemung to ten thousand for Otsego," the NYSAC Executive Director said. "I must have talked to this broker and other vendors fifteen times at all times of the day and night as we tried to fulfill the orders of these local governments. Soon, the vendors only wanted orders of one million or more. Then all of a sudden nobody would help us. We never did accomplish the bulk purchase. But in the end, Dutchess County was able to use their supplies to help any county in need."

24

The Association at Work for Counties

Just as every county official pivoted to address the pandemic, the Association representing them did as well. In addition to the county leaders' calls, they tracked local emergency orders and policies so they could be shared with other counties. Association staff developed a website devoted to federal, state, and local resources that county officials were looking for. They delivered training programs designed to support the officials as they moved from in-person meetings and operations to serving the public online.

Flattening the Curve

As part of its effort to support counties, NYSAC created three turnkey campaigns that county leaders could adapt and deploy.

The NY Counties Lead campaign was designed to bring attention to the local response to the global pandemic. NYSAC tracked county efforts to flatten the curve by lowering the rates of infection in their communities. The campaign was also used to advocate for federal funding for counties and encourage state leaders not to cut funding for counties and local governments.

Take 5 for New York and Take 5 for New York Food Banks were two different campaigns that counties could adopt to encourage social connections during the stay-at-home orders. Take 5 for New York encouraged residents to take five minutes a day to call family members, friends, and neighbors to make sure that they were OK during this unprecedented social isolation. Take 5 for New York Food Banks was based on a challenge put forth by Seneca County board members to ask residents to donate $5 or volunteer for five hours to help support local food pantries and regional food banks.

NYSAC also created three public service announcements. The first PSA, "All on the Line," was created to help launch the NY Counties Lead campaign and won national and local awards. The Telly Award-winning PSA was created by communication consultant Jon Summers with photos and video of county officials doing their jobs during the first wave of the pandemic. The second PSA, created by NYSAC's communication team, used action photos of county leaders at testing sites, handing out PPE, holding press conferences, and working in their emergency operations centers. The third PSA, produced in English and Spanish, was launched in January and designed to encourage New Yorkers to get vaccinated, and to continue taking precautions—for instance, washing hands and remaining socially distant.

The Association created a daily special bulletin to provide information on the governor's executive orders, federal actions, and other content that county officials needed to see on a more immediate timeline. NYSAC staff members monitored county executives' press conferences and tracked what counties were doing to help their communities. These were listed as one-paragraph items in daily blogs that were shared with county officials across the state.

Weekly Zoom press conferences, held by the Association, featured pairs of county executives from different regions who would talk about how their counties were working to protect their communities and also to ask federal and state elected officials for funding and resources to fight the virus.

NYSAC also used its podcast series, press releases, and social media to publicize the ways county leaders were working with their sheriffs, highway superintendents, district attorneys, 911 coordinators, solid-waste directors, social services commissioners, and others to help their residents.

Sharing Best Practices

NYSAC collected and posted the following innovative solutions that counties were implementing during the first several weeks of the public health crisis.

In March, Albany County Executive Dan McCoy

encouraged children to send e-cards to seniors. He shared examples of the electronic cards that children were sending to Shaker Place Rehabilitation & Nursing Center to put smiles on the faces of older residents. Kids were encouraged to send their cards, well wishes, and drawings to AlbanyCountyKidsCare@albanycountyny.gov.

On April 8, Broome County Executive Jason Garnar announced the launch of Operation Crush Covid. The operation mandated that people born in an even year may only go shopping, to go the park or golf on even calendar dates; people born in an odd year, could go out on odd calendar dates. This policy remained in effect through April.

In early April, the Chautauqua County Department of Health posted a list of all the grocery stores in the county that provided pick-up and delivery services and posted recipes and grocery list recommendations.

Chemung County was the first county to launch a centralized website hub of all the local restaurants that were staying open and converting to takeout online. And to help parents provide an entertainment outlet for their children, Chemung County Executive Christopher Moss held an Easter coloring contest.

In late March, Dutchess County Executive Marc Molinaro promoted the county's Mental Health Helpline, saying that it was "even more important we all support each other as best we can." Residents could call or text the helpline 24/7, and the county's mental health professionals were ready to help.

Erie County Executive Mark Poloncarz stepped up to help residents who may have lost their jobs with a campaign called Local Opportunities for Employment. The county identified and provided a one-stop list of the various businesses that were hiring during the pandemic.

Monroe County Executive Adam Bello released the Six Feet Saves campaign in mid-April in partnership with the city of Rochester, the University of Rochester, and multiple community agencies, with messaging targeting at-risk neighborhoods. The campaign included PSAs, billboards, lawn signs, and sidewalk art in English and Spanish.

Montgomery County Executive Matthew Ossenfort promoted the county's social service programs, particularly the Supplemental Nutrition Assistance Program (SNAP), throughout the beginning of the pandemic, and he also created a Neighborhood Chalk Walk campaign as part of the county's Stronger Together campaign. Families participated in the Chalk Walk over a weekend in April and shared photos of their sidewalk art with the county and on social media.

Nassau County Executive Laura Curran established a Coronavirus Economic Advisory Council to assess the countywide impact on both small and large businesses. Hofstra University supported the county and the Nassau County Industrial Development Agency to help mitigate the economic impacts of the pandemic.

On March 23, New York City Mayor Bill de Blasio announced that the city was building a citywide network to make sure food was available for those who could not afford it. According to the mayor, it would take a mobilization never seen before in New York City.

Oneida County Executive Anthony Picente, at the conclusion of his daily health briefing on Sunday, March 23, made a special request of the community to "Light a Light" on porches across the county as a tribute to all the healthcare workers who were putting themselves at risk.

Onondaga County Executive Ryan McMahon participated in a webinar series with CenterState, a local thinktank, to talk with community groups, residents, and business leaders about the immediate and potential long-term economic and public health response to the coronavirus crisis. This followed a comprehensive shelter-in-place campaign that encouraged residents to stay at home every other day.

The Orange County Office for the Aging (OFA) provided meals to homebound seniors throughout the pandemic. Seniors simply had to call the OFA. In addition, Orange County Executive Steve Neuhaus worked with a local grocery store chain to arrange for a tractor-trailer of food to be delivered to a centrally located church parking lot to help ensure residents had enough food for their families.

Putnam County Executive MaryEllen Odell ordered the establishing of a Row of Honor along Lake Gleneida in Carmel to recognize the everyday heroes, including first responders and healthcare workers, on the front lines of the pandemic. The Row of Honor of American flags will be raised each Memorial Day and Veterans Day.

Rensselaer County Executive Steve McLaughlin issued

two directives at the end of March designed to protect residents by restricting travel into the county. The directives required anyone from affected areas traveling to Rensselaer County to report to the county health department and to quarantine for fourteen days.

In Rockland County, the Masked Warriors Project began sewing homemade masks and providing them to hospitals, frontline workers, and departments in the county. The group was working with Rockland County Executive Ed Day and with the hospitals to develop safe and effective distribution network.

At the end of March, Suffolk County Executive Steve Bellone shifted the county's response from containment to a mitigation strategy to better direct resources as the coronavirus spread throughout the county. This strategy included a new policy to begin rear boarding for Suffolk County transit to help protect drivers. The county encouraged everyone to avoid using cash on buses and instead to download the mobile fare app.

Immediately upon closure of nonessential businesses, Ulster County created the unique Project Resilience campaign to provide restaurant meals to households throughout the county, free of charge, while simultaneously providing restaurants much needed revenue to stay afloat. Early in the pandemic, the project provided well over twenty thousand meals and raised over $2.2 million in contributions for the program.

By March 24, the Westchester County Department of Social Services (DSS) had changed the way it provided services to prevent the spread of coronavirus. As a precaution, in-person contact was eliminated whenever possible, with DSS transitioning to offer assistance by phone to reduce the potential for virus exposure. Those in need of benefits could apply online, and applications could also be mailed or faxed to DSS.

25

Tip of the Spear—The Local Public Health Response

County public health officials were among the unsung heroes of the COVID-19 pandemic. In every community across New York, they were the ones who donned personal protective equipment and faced off against the largest and most aggressive global public health crisis in a century. These public servants work for county local health departments (LHDs) that have been decimated by ten years of funding cuts by New York State and the federal government.

LHDs operate under the statutory authority of Article 3 and Article 6 of New York State's Public Health Law. They provide core public health services and put the state's public health prevention agenda into action at the local level.

Traditionally, local public health experts diagnose and provide for the health of each community by tracking general health statistics of community residents. They investigate everything that affects the health of a population or a neighborhood—like food, water, and air—to prevent health problems before they start. They conduct community health assessments to identify health needs and disparities, and they manage inspections and permitting of regulated facilities, such as restaurants and summer camps, to prevent widespread community sickness.

Public health departments work with schools, businesses, government agencies, hospitals, pharmacies, not-for-profit organizations, and faith communities to foster collective action for overall community health. They are the governmental entities charged and trained to be the frontline workers in any of a full range of emergencies. In New York, LHDs are the only entities with legal responsibility under Article 6 of Public Health Law for communicable disease control, health emergency preparedness and response, and municipal immunization programs.

Local health departments receive funding from a number of sources, including county property tax and sales tax revenue; fees; fines; reimbursement for services; state aid for general public health work (known as Article 6 funding); and state, federal and private grants. Isn't it shortsighted that the local government agencies most critical to protecting New Yorkers during this pandemic have faced funding cuts in state and federal budgets for more than a decade?

At the federal level, Congress had consistently cut public health funding. According to NACo, our nation's public system lost twenty-five thousand jobs and a quarter of our public health infrastructure since 2008. Instead of maintaining consistent levels of funding for public health services, Congress funded local public health from crisis to crisis. "They dedicated money for Zika. They dedicated money for H1N1. They dedicated money to Hep C. They dedicated money to HIV," said NACo Executive Director Matt Chase. "But this did not allow local leaders to prepare their local infrastructure or build a strong public health response network."

At the state level, budget cuts were partially responsible for the layoffs, attrition, and hiring freezes that had reduced local health department staffing by 33 percent since 2011. These funding cuts had made it more difficult for LHDs to hire, train, and retain the experts needed to respond to this pandemic. As a result, along with the magnitude of the impact of COVID-19, counties have had to reassign public health staff from core public health services to pandemic response activities and bring in employees from other county agencies. These challenges impacted the morale of LHD staff and leaders, who have had little time off, saw scores of their colleagues retire early, and witnessed the personal impact of COVID-19 on friends, family, colleagues, and community members.

COVID-19 Comes to New York State

On January 17, when the first two U.S. COVID-19 cases were confirmed in Washington state and California, the

New York State Department of Health issued guidance for healthcare facilities and workers encountering any patient with symptoms of the new infectious disease. A week later, NYSDOH hosted its first weekly COVID-19 webinar for healthcare providers and LHDs, detailing clinical updates about this new disease that was primarily spread person to person through small respiratory droplets and could be transmitted by asymptomatic carriers.

In early February, as state and local health departments continued preparing for the potential widespread transmission of COVID-19 in New York, the United States suspended most flights from China, where the virus originated, and the entry of foreign nationals who had traveled to China within the past fourteen days. While officials were concerned about travelers from Asia bringing the virus into the country, a study by Icahn School of Medicine at Mount Sinai published in the journal *Science* later showed that low-level circulation of COVID-19 in New York City had begun in early February through untracked transmission between the United States and Europe.

The pandemic did not, however, attract the attention of the public in New York until March 1, when a patient in New Rochelle, Westchester County, tested positive for COVID-19. This patient had been deemed a "superspreader," meaning that he could transmit the virus to a high number of people.

Governor Cuomo took a number of decisive actions in the following days: waiving co-pays for COVID-19 tests on March 2; signing a $40 million emergency management authorization for the state's coronavirus response on March 3, which gave him broad executive powers to issue directives; and activating a statewide Emergency Operation Center in Albany with two outposts in Westchester on March 5.

On March 7, with a total of eighty-nine cases across the state, the governor declared a state of emergency, which gave him the unilateral power to expedite the procurement of personal protective equipment and testing and medical supplies, expand the field of professionals permitted to test residents for the virus, and initiate his extraordinary executive powers granted by the State Legislature.

Over the following weeks, K-12 and university students moved to remote learning; gathering sizes were limited, and then limited again; visits to nursing homes and prisons were banned; nonessential workers were sent to work from home; bars and restaurants were closed to indoor dining; movie theaters, gyms, and casinos were shuttered; and New York's economy, recreation, and social activities were put on PAUSE.

On March 14, an eighty-two-year-old Brooklyn woman with emphysema died. This was the first COVID-19 death in New York.

Supporting the Public Health Response

Both initially and throughout the pandemic, contact tracing was the key focus for local health departments. With several decades of experience in contact tracing, LHDs set to work identifying the contacts of confirmed COVID-19 cases and organizing logistics to provide the basic necessities that individuals needed under quarantine or isolation, such as housing and food.

While LHDs relied on their own contact tracing staff and cross-trained employees from other county agencies, on April 22, Governor Cuomo and former New York City Mayor Michael R. Bloomberg launched a statewide contact tracing program in partnership with New Jersey and Connecticut. As part of the effort, the Johns Hopkins Bloomberg School of Public Health built an online curriculum and training program for candidates recruited by NYSDOH and Bloomberg Philanthropies. Meanwhile, the global public health organization Vital Strategies developed call-center protocols and digital tools. The program was funded with $10.5 million from the Bloomberg Philanthropies and $1.3 billion from the federal government. The program was projected to train at least thirty contact tracers per hundred thousand New York State residents, as advised in the CDC guidelines.

By July 15, the NYS Contact Tracing Program touted an 86 percent success rate in reaching and interviewing COVID-19 positive New Yorkers, according to a Cuomo advisor overseeing the effort.

From the beginning, the availability of COVID-19 testing proved a monumental challenge for New York's pandemic response. To increase testing accessibility, Governor Cuomo issued an executive order on April 12 expanding the eligibility of workers permitted to conduct COVID-19 diagnostic and antibody tests. At a press conference three days later, he prioritized healthcare providers, first responders, and essential workers for testing.

Knowing the state would first have to tackle the unreliability of the testing reagent supply chain, NYSDOH announced on April 17 its intention to establish a single, statewide coordinating testing prioritization process for all in-state labs. LHDs did their part by working with local providers, hospitals, federally qualified health centers, businesses, congregate settings, and other entities to direct them to available testing, administer testing in some cases, and advocate for greater testing and laboratory capacity.

The state launched large-scale antibody testing in late April to help determine what percentage of the population had been exposed to the virus. This was meant to facilitate the state's reopening by determining the percentage of the population that was plausibly immune to the virus and could safely return to work. It began by conducting tests over a two-day period at grocery stores and other shopping areas. NYSDOH collected three thousand samples from forty locations in nineteen counties. The prevalence of antibodies ranged widely, from 3.6 percent in most upstate counties to 21.1 percent in New York City. It was clear that most New Yorkers had not been exposed to the virus and it was not safe to reopen.

Meanwhile, the state continued revising its diagnostic testing criteria to become more inclusive until July 1, when it opened testing to all New Yorkers, having already conducted four million tests in total.

While serving as the frontline public health responders

to the pandemic, LHDs also continued their core public health work in community outreach and education, providing scientific information, sharing daily updates about the outbreak and the local community impact, and offering recommendations for how best to protect one's family from exposure. As New York moved to reopen through the summer months, LHDs led the local outreach to businesses and the public on state, social-distancing measures designed to prevent a resurgence of disease and led the local enforcement of the governor's executive orders.

Curbing the Powers of the LHD

While New York's Public Health Law and the State Sanitary Code assign primary control of disease outbreak management to LHDs and county health officials, the state health commissioner has the power to step in and take a more active role when local interventions require additional support. That authority was exerted on April 17 when Governor Cuomo issued an executive order that declared, "No local government or local department of health shall take any actions that could affect public health without consulting with the state department of health" and "no local government official shall take any action that could impede or conflict with any other local government actions, or state actions, with respect to managing the COVID-19 public health emergency."

LHDs and local governments remained responsible for enforcement of the governor's directives but struggled with implementing the changing executive orders, and delays in guidance made it difficult to operationalize new public health measures.

Supporting the Reopening

In mid-May, as the disease curve flattened and positive cases, hospitalizations, and deaths decreased, Governor Cuomo developed a four-phase regional reopening plan, assigning certain businesses and services to each phase. The plan allowed for time to assess the impact of the reopening of various businesses and services based on case numbers. Regions had to meet and monitor specific metrics to move through each phase.

To help promote an accurate count of cases, each region was required to conduct at least thirty tests for every one thousand residents. By May 5, one million New Yorkers had been tested and, by May 22, more than 670 testing sites were operating statewide. The Finger Lakes, Southern Tier, and Mohawk Valley were the first regions to meet the metrics to reopen and entered Phase I of reopening on May 15. New York City was the last region to reopen, entering Phase 1 on June 8.

Helping Businesses, Schools, and Healthcare Facilities

While LHDs were not officially responsible for approving business reopening plans, they were actively involved in the local reopening process. They received many inquiries and spent countless hours helping businesses follow state guidance.

LHDs also had to enforce the state's guidelines for the reopening of businesses such as bars, restaurants, outdoor entertainment gatherings, summer camps, and gyms. Full-service LHDs dedicated significant time and resources to investigating complaints about noncompliant businesses and initiating a dialogue with offenders.

The reopening of gym and fitness centers imposed a unique responsibility on LHDs, with the state requiring LHDs to inspect each one before it could reopen. These facilities were not previously regulated by LHDs and now required local partnerships between code enforcement, fire marshals, and heating, ventilation, and air conditioning providers to ensure that gyms and fitness centers met all the mandated protective facility changes.

In the middle of the summer of 2020, LHDs shifted part of their focus to helping K-12 schools and colleges and universities reopen. Both settings posed unique challenges and each had specific state requirements designed to reduce the risk of disease transmission. Local health departments provided technical support and coordination to develop plans that addressed social distancing measures, cleaning and disinfecting, and the actions and communication processes that would be taken when COVID cases occurred in school and campus settings.

Throughout the pandemic response, LHDs worked closely with hospitals and healthcare providers. In the first wave of the pandemic, they helped ensure that healthcare workers were properly supplied with PPE and, if they weren't, that they received new supplies first.

Battling a Second Wave and Deploying the Vaccines

In response to a growing number of case clusters, on November 17, Governor Cuomo announced that the state would be deploying a new "micro-cluster" control strategy that focused on geographically limited closures and testing requirements in schools designed to identify and quickly control disease hotspots. LHDs engaged with schools and community healthcare partners to support the new testing capacity, resources, staffing, and laboratory requirements that would be needed to address the state's response criteria.

Just as these clusters were growing across the state, the first two vaccines from Pfizer and Moderna were approved at the end of November and the first shipments were delivered to states in early December. The first New Yorker was vaccinated against COVID-19 on December 14.

The first round of Phase 1 vaccines in New York State was limited to high-risk hospital workers, nursing home residents, and nursing home staff. The Centers for Disease Control and Prevention also launched a program called the Pharmacy Partnership for Long-Term Care Program for COVID-19, under which employees of CVS, Walgreens, and other select pharmacies vaccinated residents and staff in nursing homes and other long-term care facilities.

New York State then expanded its massive vaccine

distribution chain to state-operated points of dispensing (PODs), local health departments, Federally Qualified Healthcare Facilities, and other healthcare providers as more demographic groups became eligible for the vaccine under the CDC's guidelines. Almost from the beginning, there was not enough supply of the vaccine to meet demand. There were had more distributors and more New Yorkers who wanted the vaccine than the federal government or the manufacturers could provide.

By mid-January, a second wave of infections was ripping through communities. The number of positive cases nearly doubled in most counties from the middle of November to the middle of December, and nearly doubled again between December and January. New strains of the virus were discovered and spreading through England and Africa, and then in a handful of counties in New York. The governor was warning of new stresses on hospitals across the state.

Counties were once again being called upon to take action to reduce the spread and assist with the distribution of new coronavirus vaccines. LHDs implemented local Points of Dispensing to vaccinate essential workers, including police, firefighters, teachers, and EMS and other frontline workers. The lack of vaccines required local health workers to spend more time responding to community questions and concerns than immunizing people. County leaders, meanwhile, lobbied state and federal representatives for a larger supply.

26

The Economic Impact of COVID-19

As New York became the epicenter of the pandemic, it was clear that the human and financial toll would be dramatic. The steps necessary to stop the spread of COVID-19 required extensive public restrictions. In addition to the public health costs of this crisis, the economy was hit in significant ways as government regulations shut down local businesses and tourism, severely impacted underemployed New Yorkers, and crippled state, county, and local government sales tax revenues.

There were personal economic effects, such as loss of income due to sickness and death, inability to pay for housing, and lost work time of caregivers and of parents with children out of school. Consumption dropped as a result of lower incomes, forced shutdowns of restaurants and businesses, restrictions on travel and mass gatherings, and fear of social contact. Restaurants and industries related to tourism, recreation, and the arts were hit especially hard.

To get ahead of the economic injury and to position the counties for the impact, NYSAC produced a series of economic reports that highlighted the impact on county sales tax revenues and economic activity by county and industrial sector. These reports indicated that businesses, local taxpayers, and county budgets were facing challenges on numerous fronts with no certainty as to how long the pandemic and related restrictions would remain in place.

- Businesses in most sectors of the economy faced an interruption in their operations. Some were completely shut down for an extended period of time.
- Small businesses that faced significant losses were forced to cut jobs to reduce costs.
- Counties faced an increased demand for public health, public safety, and human services during a recession.
- Counties faced a loss in critical local sales tax revenues from lost economic activity.
- The state imposed enacted hundreds of millions of dollars in identified state reimbursement cuts at the beginning of the pandemic as its own fiscal picture darkened with a projected $15 billion deficit. In addition, the adopted state budget outlined further undefined cuts that the governor indicated could reach as high as 50 percent in some state line items.
- Residents saw significant reductions to local quality of life services.

New York on PAUSE

Early in the pandemic, broad statewide steps were taken, with all corners of New York essentially being treated the same and subject to similar limitations. Several of the first series of executive orders imposed by the governor focused on closing down all facets of the economy and social interaction.

These early EOs that limited business activity would be referred to as "New York State on PAUSE," directing all nonessential businesses to close their in-person operations and banning all nonessential gatherings of individuals of any size for any reason. These EOs closed schools and all places of public amusement—malls, museums, amusement rides, carnivals, aquariums, zoos, arcades, fairs, public parks, theme parks, water parks, children's play centers, funplexes, bowling alleys, family and children's attractions. All businesses that attracted people that could not adequately social distance were closed. Through December 2020, many restrictions remained in place that limited density in places of business and office buildings, and numerous performing arts and entertainment venues remained shuttered.

Many of the state's business leaders did not want to close. They requested exemptions from the EOs. Local business owners, meanwhile, were contacting county leaders, asking them if they could be exempted at the local level. Counties did not have that authority.

As more data became available, the governor gradually reduced restrictions on a regional basis using a variety of public health data points: virus cases, hospitalizations, and ICU capacity. NY-PAUSE began on March 21 and ended in most regions on May 15, with other regional economies opening in the following three weeks, based on their infection rate.

Tracking the Fiscal Impact

Throughout the pandemic, there was little hard data available to model the financial impact. New York's counties decided it was essential to develop their own impact estimates and to monitor the results.

At the first appearance of the virus in New York, NYSAC asked a former state budget official and economist to help develop a model to estimate the potential impact of the pandemic on economic activity and on local sales tax revenues. Sales tax is a key revenue source for most counties, and the one that would be most impacted by the slowing of consumer activity. NYSAC's report provided an overall forecasting framework to measure the financial impact on counties; the methodology also served to project the losses by the different segments of New York's economy.

Sales Tax

The initial report began with a review of studies by economists, financial experts, and municipal finance officials of recent economic downturns, including the Great

Recession. This included employment trends, the potential impact of government-imposed restrictions on travel and mass gatherings and determining which taxable industries would be hurt the most by these restrictions. This was followed by an analysis of the general response of the public to the virus and their comfort level with participating in "regular" economic activity.

The initial focus was on industries that would be most impacted by travel and density restrictions. Under this model, during a mild recession, the report assumed taxable sales would decline, on average, by 40 percent for restaurants, hotels, bars, and other tourism related industries. These reductions are in full effect for one full quarter, after which restrictions begin to ease in the ensuing three quarters. The table on the next page provides more details on the methodology used in the initial report.

Sales Tax Impact by Category[1] - Year 1

Industrial Group	Mild	Severe
Other	-10.0%	-20.0%
Arts & Recreation	-40.0%	-80.0%
Auto Related	-15.0%	-30.0%
Restuarants & Other Eating Establishments	-40.0%	-80.0%
Gasoline Stations	-20.0%	-40.0%
Health Related	-2.5%	-5.0%
Travel Accommodation (& Occupancy Tax)	-40.0%	-80.0%
General Retail	-15.0%	-30.0%
Grocery	-10.0%	-20.0%
Transportation/Trade	-33.5%	-67.0%

Table 1: [1] Reductions are from a baseline. Source data is Tax and Finance total taxable sales database.

Initial forecasts assumed all industries were hit equally across the state; that is, a restaurant in Dutchess County would be impacted the same as one in New York City. It was anticipated that over time the impact would vary regionally depending on the intensity of the pandemic in each area. By the end of 2020, it was clear that New York City along with larger downstate counties would bear the brunt of the economic impacts, but all regions of the state had deeply impacted counties.

The New York City Traveler Accommodation-based taxable sales were down by 90 percent from March through November, and Restaurant and Other Eating Places taxable sales were down about 59 percent compared to the prior year. On an annual basis, nearly 20 percent of New York City's taxable sales come from these two categories. In many other counties and regions, these two industries were also down considerably with traveler accommodations down in the range of 30 to 60 percent and restaurants down in twenty to 40 percent on average, over the same time.

A Steep Drop in Economic Activity

The period of March through May represented the deepest trough of the pandemic and included the most significant restrictions on economic activity. Taxable sales activity for this period was a staggering $25 billion lower than the prior year, down nearly 28 percent. All taxable sales data is reported before any diversion of local sales tax by the state or local revenue sharing arrangements. Table 2 on the following page summarizes taxable sales data by industrial (NAICS) category for the March-April-May 2020 period compared to 2019. Taxable sales represent the full value of the transaction, not the sales tax generated.

NYS Taxable Sales, March through May 2020 -- Year over Year Comparison

Rank	Description	TTS 2019 March to May		Rank	Description	TTS 2020 March to May	Year over Year $ Change	Year over Year % Change
1	Restaurants and Other Eating Places	$10,492,090,247		1	Electronic Shopping and Mail-Order Houses	$5,417,954,926	$3,087,164,979	132.50%
2	Automobile Dealers	$8,267,272,778		2	Automobile Dealers	$4,657,114,045	($3,610,158,733)	-43.70%
3	Building Material and Supplies Dealers	$3,897,470,632		3	Restaurants and Other Eating Places	$4,426,486,969	($6,065,603,278)	-57.80%
4	Traveler Accommodation	$3,112,329,450		4	Building Material and Supplies Dealers	$3,771,363,586	($126,107,046)	-3.20%
5	Gen. Merch. Stores, Warehouses & Supercenters	$3,069,042,553		5	Gen. Merch. Stores, Warehouses & Supercenters	$3,172,718,604	$103,676,051	3.40%
6	Gasoline Stations	$3,029,585,054		6	Grocery Stores	$2,513,768,913	($23,914,485)	-0.90%
7	Grocery Stores	$2,537,683,398		7	Gasoline Stations	$2,259,264,113	($770,320,941)	-25.40%
8	Electronic Shopping and Mail-Order Houses	$2,330,789,947		8	Electric Power Gen./Transmission & Dist.	$1,801,963,384	($55,918,480)	-3.00%
9	Other Miscellaneous Store Retailers	$2,249,069,025		9	Wired & Wireless Telecommunications Carriers	$1,716,182,990	($249,738,417)	-12.70%
10	Clothing Stores	$2,200,300,016		10	Other Information Services	$1,516,955,647	$696,210,857	84.80%
11	Wired & Wireless Telecommunications Carriers	$1,965,921,407		11	Other Miscellaneous Store Retailers	$1,440,387,780	($808,681,245)	-36.00%
12	Electric Power Gen./Transmission & Dist.	$1,857,881,864		12	Computer Systems Design & Related Services	$1,371,601,499	$106,239,467	8.40%
13	Administration of Economic Programs	$1,571,360,476		13	Beer, Wine, and Liquor Stores	$1,345,464,512	$275,944,005	25.80%
14	Automotive Repair and Maintenance	$1,552,570,748		14	Services to Buildings and Dwellings	$1,274,625,966	($195,890,462)	-13.30%
15	Services to Buildings and Dwellings	$1,470,516,428		15	Software Publishers	$1,065,483,119	$106,657,110	10.00%
16	Health and Personal Care Stores	$1,395,640,969		16	Other Prof., Scientific, and Technical Services	$1,047,524,889	($113,636,767)	-9.80%
17	Computer Systems Design & Related Services	$1,265,362,032		17	Automotive Repair and Maintenance	$1,036,728,113	($515,842,635)	-33.20%
18	Electronics and Appliance Stores	$1,200,412,992		18	Health and Personal Care Stores	$1,024,223,334	($371,417,635)	-26.60%
19	Other Prof., Scientific, and Technical Services	$1,161,161,656		19	Building Equipment Contractors	$838,323,489	($241,564,974)	-22.40%
20	Building Equipment Contractors	$1,079,888,463		20	Computer & Peripheral Equip. Manufacturing	$837,358,765	($44,868,721)	-5.10%
	Top 20	$55,706,350,135			Top 20	$42,535,494,643	($13,170,855,492)	-23.6%
	TTS March-April-May 2019	$90,355,233,944			TTS March-April-May 2020	$65,410,640,364	($24,944,593,580)	-27.6%
	Top 20 as Share of Total Taxable Sales	61.7%			Top 20 as Share of Total Taxable Sales	65.0%		

The June through August period provided improvements in taxable sales activity in many regions of the state as sectors of the economy gradually reopened beginning in the latter half of May. Statewide, total taxable sales were down about $8.6 billion in the June through August period, or about -9 percent year over year. While still down overall, this represented an improvement over the prior quarter, and thirty-eight counties saw taxable sales activity meet or exceed the 2019 levels for the June through August period. Table 3 highlights the statewide results for June through August.

NYS Taxable Sales, June through August 2020 -- Year over Year Comparison

		Q2 2019			Q2 2020		
Rank	Description	June - August	Rank	Description	June - August	$ Change	% Change
1	Restaurants and Other Eating Places	$10,837,257,886	1	Automobile Dealers	$9,174,071,929	$673,814,131	7.9%
2	Automobile Dealers	$8,500,257,798	2	Restaurants and Other Eating Places	$6,562,413,050	($4,274,844,836)	-39.4%
3	Building Material and Supplies Dealers	$4,065,840,941	3	Electronic Shopping and Mail-Order Houses	$6,006,096,156	$3,442,964,118	134.3%
4	Traveler Accommodation	$3,524,843,652	4	Building Material and Supplies Dealers	$4,772,788,410	$706,947,469	17.4%
5	Gasoline Stations	$3,276,292,102	5	Gen. Merch. Stores, Warehouse Clubs & Supercenters	$3,564,788,250	$288,554,678	8.8%
6	Gen. Merch. Stores, Warehouse Clubs & Supercenters	$3,276,233,572	6	Gasoline Stations	$2,974,872,435	($301,419,667)	-9.2%
7	Grocery Stores	$2,709,268,304	7	Grocery Stores	$2,676,988,584	($32,279,720)	-1.2%
8	Electronic Shopping and Mail-Order Houses	$2,563,132,038	8	Other Miscellaneous Store Retailers	$2,011,606,292	$81,310,204	4.2%
9	Electric Power Gen., Transmission & Distribution	$2,060,878,579	9	Electric Power Gen., Transmission & Distribution	$1,965,839,212	($95,039,367)	-4.6%
10	Clothing Stores	$2,029,578,564	10	Administration of Economic Programs	$1,881,911,544	$298,701,143	18.9%
11	Other Miscellaneous Store Retailers	$1,930,296,088	11	Wired and Wireless Telecommunications Carriers	$1,725,708,126	($199,400,082)	-10.4%
12	Wired and Wireless Telecommunications Carriers	$1,925,108,208	12	Other Information Services	$1,581,543,964	$266,012,494	20.2%
13	Services to Buildings and Dwellings	$1,615,460,201	13	Services to Buildings and Dwellings	$1,466,279,707	($149,180,494)	-9.2%
14	Automotive Repair and Maintenance	$1,614,413,314	14	Automotive Repair and Maintenance	$1,463,191,077	($151,222,237)	-9.4%
15	Office Administrative Services	$1,588,682,306	15	Beer, Wine, and Liquor Stores	$1,407,787,668	$278,244,731	24.6%
16	Administration of Economic Programs	$1,583,210,401	16	Computer Systems Design and Related Services	$1,338,425,710	$36,176,303	2.8%
17	Health and Personal Care Stores	$1,365,254,364	17	Clothing Stores	$1,227,537,624	($802,040,940)	-39.5%
18	Other Information Services	$1,315,531,470	18	Software Publishers	$1,222,544,859	$231,095,204	23.3%
19	Computer Systems Design and Related Services	$1,302,249,407	19	Electronics and Appliance Stores	$1,164,130,028	($107,823,979)	-8.5%
20	Electronics and Appliance Stores	$1,271,954,007	20	Health and Personal Care Stores	$1,115,849,065	($249,405,299)	-18.3%
	Top 20	$58,355,743,202		Top 20	$55,304,373,690	($3,051,369,512)	-5.2%
	TTS 2019 June-July-August	$95,038,939,731		TTS 2020 June-July-August	$86,442,136,194	($8,596,803,537)	-9.0%
	Top 20 as Share of Total Taxable Sales	61.4%		Top 20 as Share of Total Taxable Sales	64.0%		

Based on the sales tax data presented by the State Department of Taxation and Finance, nearly every business sector saw major declines in sales activities, led by travel accommodations, restaurants, clothing stores, and appliances. The sectors that did not see declines were internet sales; beer, wine, and liquor; and software related businesses.

How the Economic Slowdown Impacted Counties

The core of county government revenues come from economic transactions. For the average county, most locally derived revenues come from a handful of sources.

- 35 percent from property tax
- 30 percent from sales tax
- 17 percent from the use and sale of property, and mortgage recording, hotel, and gaming taxes
- 17 percent from charges for services

Counties rely on sales tax as their primary revenue source, with more than one-third having sales tax as their top source of revenue. Property taxes are important, but the annual growth has been capped under state law since 2012. Counties received state and federal aid, but those funds are highly restricted as reimbursement for an expense the county incurred on behalf of the state or federal government.

Counties rely on local revenues to provide essential

services, including many services critical to combatting the virus, such as public health, social services, emergency operations center activities, public safety, and public works. Any dramatic disruption to county revenue streams has significant consequences for fighting the virus and helping local businesses.

As indicated above, at the beginning of New York's PAUSE order, NYSAC released an initial projection of how the virus could impact economic activity and how that may impact county sales tax revenues. In the initial March report, the expected impact ranged from a $350 million annual loss in local sales tax revenue (-4 percent) to more than $1 billion (-12.3 percent). A month later, the data showed an impact that was staggeringly worse. The sales tax collected for April was down about 28 percent in total for the month compared to the prior year, a range from about -19 percent to -40 percent by county.

By May, as more data became available, under the milder scenario, the projection for sales tax losses outside New York City was increased to show a total drop of about 9 percent, for a loss of about $780 million. Under the more severe scenario, total sales tax losses were projected to drop 22 percent.

Counties braced for significant losses. And they came. Aggregate sales tax losses for the COVID months of March through the first part of December were significant, compounding to $2.2 billion from the expected baseline when budgets were enacted, a drop of 16 percent for the ten months alone. However, as the year progressed, it was clear that New York City and about two dozen counties would bear most of the losses due to the nature of their local economies that relied more on the businesses most impacted by density restrictions. Other counties were able to meet their sales tax numbers for the year. The chart provides a breakdown of actual revenue declines during the COVID months in 2020 compared to collections during the same period in 2019.

57 Counties & New York City				
	2020	**2019**	**$ Change**	**%Change**
March	$1,393,502,206	$1,446,618,690	($53,116,485)	-3.7%
April	$935,210,009	$1,236,519,785	($301,309,776)	-24.4%
May	$845,692,129	$1,247,285,349	($401,593,219)	-32.2%
June	$1,265,919,570	$1,674,719,898	($408,800,327)	-24.4%
July	$1,201,119,339	$1,307,800,653	($106,681,314)	-8.2%
August	$1,213,818,260	$1,314,512,832	($100,694,571)	-7.7%
September	$1,550,970,926	$1,735,804,001	($184,833,075)	-10.6%
October	$1,254,900,084	$1,323,327,736	($68,427,652)	-5.2%
November	$1,241,865,287	$1,335,844,812	($93,979,525)	-7.0%
December	$1,569,862,005	$1,698,962,604	($129,100,599)	-7.6%
COVID Months	**$12,472,859,815**	**$14,321,396,358**	**($1,848,536,543)**	**-12.9%**

Table 4: Gross sales tax before any state diversions ($59.1 million in 2020) and sales tax sharing.

Westchester County sales tax rate increased from 3 percent to 4 percent on August 1, 2019. No adjustments have been made to recognize the rate change. NYSAC estimates cash receipts would be about $91 million lower if adjusted for the rate change.

Economic Activity Increased in Phases

It is important to note the timing of the key pandemic events, including lockdown and reopening dates, to get a better understanding of why taxable sales improved in different regions of the state during the June through August period.

- March 1 – First positive COVID-19 case in New York State.
- March 21 – NY-PAUSE began.

The goal of NY Paus was to limit the spread of the virus through density reduction and restricting high-risk activities. Essential businesses and activities were defined by the state. PAUSE remained in place until May 15 when certain regions of the state began a phased reopening in this order.

- May 15 (Finger Lakes, North Country, Southern Tier, Central New York, and Mohawk Valley)
- May 19 (Western New York)
- May 20 (Capital Region)
- May 26 (Hudson Valley)
- May 27 (Long Island)
- June 8 (New York City)

As Phase 1 reopenings occurred by region, sales activity changed modestly but remained far below prior year levels. Each new phase allowed for more economic activity with fewer restrictions. Typically, if a region met required public health metrics it was allowed to move on to the next phase of reopening after a two-week period. New York City was the last region to enter Phase 4 on June 8.

By August, it was clear that the depth of the downturn would be longer and deeper than initially forecast for some regions of the state. The data confirmed that, in aggregate, the pandemic would impact local government receipts and spending over multiple budget years, and that some regions of the state would be more greatly impacted for a longer period.

Throughout the pandemic, counties struggled with mounting, unbudgeted COVID-related costs and lost sales tax revenue because of the reduced economic transactions stemming from the PAUSE. Counties also faced state funding cuts as the state struggled with revenue shortfalls, particularly in its income, sales, and profits-based taxes. The state's financial plan projected a shortfall of $13.3 billion in the 2020–21 state fiscal year (the year of the pandemic) and indicated that, without additional federal support to help replace lost revenues, state aid to counties would be cut by 20 to 50 percent. At 20 percent these cuts translated to a loss of $635 million for programs the county already delivered and paid for, though this did not include New York City.

An updated State Financial Plan released in late October for the halfway point in the state fiscal year indicated that its budget gap had widened slightly in each of the out years of the plan from 2022 through 2024, suggesting that these state cuts in local assistance would be made permanent to address shortfalls at the state level.

While other state governments had shared their Coronavirus Relief Funding with the counties in their states, New York did not share any of the $5.2 billion it received from the CARES Act.

So while counties were struggling financially and urging Congress to provide direct funding, the state cut local aid, intercepted local sales tax revenue, and refused to share federal CARES Act funding with them.

Keeping Counties Afloat

There were three things keeping counties afloat through the pandemic. The first was prudent budgeting from prior years to build up rainy day funds. Second was adapting their spending at the beginning of the public health crisis. Third was a lifeline from Congress in the form of increased federal Medicaid funding. As soon as the pandemic was declared and the economy was shut down, most counties began cutting expenses. Counties eliminated staff, ended service contracts, deferred, or even scrapped capital expenses, and shored up their finances however possible.

The other boost for counties was the enhanced Federal Medicaid Assistance Percentage (eFMAP) included in the federal stimulus package signed by the president on March 18. Over a full year, this funding is expected to generate over $4 billion for New York State, and about $160 million for counties for each quarter of the declared state of emergency— $95 million in savings for New York City and $65 million for the rest of the state. Through March 2021, counties and New York City had saved approximately $655 million.

Uncertainty Reigns

Scientists and public health professionals learned much about the virus since it first appeared. Yet much remained unknown even as 2020 came to a close. A second wave of infections was growing across the country and showing up in hotspots around New York. A new, much more contagious strain identified in the United Kingdom was turning up in communities across the state beginning in early 2021. The growth of infections and hospitalizations was happening just as the state and counties were adapting new plans to distribute as many vaccines as possible to tiered categories of New Yorkers, beginning with healthcare professionals and front-line workers.

This new spike of infections was present in many parts of the world, causing a new round of economic restrictions from full shutdowns to limits to the number of people allowed in stores, restaurants, and business offices. As 2021 began, there was a race between slowing the spread, vaccinating enough people to create herd immunity, and keeping the economy active enough to forestall a prolonged recession.

The New Year Brings Hope

Counties reacted to the fiscal uncertainty of the COVID-19 pandemic by quickly controlling the costs they could and laying the groundwork for a more stable 2021 budget season. Counties had little choice. There was no way to know how long and deep the recession caused by the pandemic would last or how quickly following public health protocols and vaccine administration would curtail the spread of the virus.

By March 1, 2021, one year after the first COVID-19 case was identified in New York State, the fiscal situation had improved dramatically for many counties since the depth of the crisis in the spring of 2020. More than half the counties closed out 2020 with sales tax receipts that met or exceeded what they collected in 2019 (but many still fell short of budgeted growth). For those that fell short, it appears that their recovery will not occur until life returns to normal; they are simply too reliant on normal travel, whether it be tourists or workers commuting to their jobs across county lines.

Even the state budget situation improved with outyear budget gaps being cut in half from earlier projections. The stronger than anticipated state revenue outlook, along with federal assistance provided to the state, allowed the Governor to limit the state reimbursement cut in 2020 to 5 percent rather than the 20 percent or more first anticipated. The introduced state budget for state fiscal year 2022 proposes to make that 5 percent state reimbursement cut permanent.

A key development during the pandemic that helped bolster economic activity was trillions of dollars in federal government stimulus payments to individuals and businesses that helped people who lost their jobs continue to pay their bills and put food on the table. This was reinforced by trillions of dollars in accommodative monetary policy from the Federal Reserve that maintained markets. However, even with these unprecedented actions, more than 20 million Americans were out of work a year later, including more than two million New Yorkers. For these folks, it appeared the pandemic must be put far behind us to restore their personal economy.

Appendix A

Federal Stimulus Laws

Throughout the pandemic, New York State's county leaders lobbied their members of Congress for funding to offset revenues lost from the economic shutdown and to help cover the increased costs of fighting the pandemic.

For a full year, from March 2020 through March 2021, two different Congresses enacted six stimulus packages designed to help the country through the pandemic. The following measures were focused on cash provided to individuals; increased unemployment benefits; the Paycheck Protection Program to help small businesses continue to pay their employees, rent, and utilities; aid to schools and colleges; funding for personal protection equipment; increased federal Medicaid funding; and funding for states, counties and local government.

Coronavirus Preparedness and Response Supplemental Appropriations Act of 2020 (H.R. 6074)

This $8.3 billion dollar package, signed into law on March 6, 2020, provided $2.2 billion in public health funding to support prevention, preparedness and response efforts, including $1 billion for Public Health Emergency Preparedness (PHEP) grants to support states, counties, cities, and tribes. The bill included $3 billion in funding for research and development for coronavirus vaccines and diagnostic tools, and $100 million in supplemental appropriations for Community Health Centers (CHC). The bill also included $3.1 billion in funding to support the Public Health and Social Service Emergency Fund under the U.S. Department of Health and Human Services.

Families First Coronavirus Response Act (H.R. 6201)

Signed into Law on March 18, 2020, this legislation included five main provisions meant to respond to the deepening crisis caused by the coronavirus outbreak: support for free testing, food assistance, enhanced Federal Medical Assistance Percentage (eFMAP) for states, unemployment aid, and paid sick and medical benefits. The legislation increased, or enhanced, from 50 percent to 56.2 percent the FMAP that the federal government provides to state and counties for Medicaid programs. This temporary increase prevented states from cutting Medicaid benefits during the pandemic. It also required states to maintain eligibility standards that are no less restrictive than the date of enactment and to maintain a special provision that preserved the existing FMAP sharing arrangements between states and their political subdivisions. This was a major victory for New York's counties, which pay $7.5 billion of the state's Medicaid program.

The Coronavirus Aid, Relief, and Economic Securities Act (CARES Act) (H.R. 748)

This measure, which was signed into law on March 27, 2020, was the largest stimulus package. It provided a federal appropriation of close to $2 trillion in federal stimulus funding. The legislation included the creation of a $415 billion Coronavirus Relief Fund, supplying large communities, including counties with a population greater than five hundred thousand residents, with federal relief to aid in COVID-19 response efforts. This legislation also extended the expiration of the federal TANF program and provided $45 billion for FEMA's Disaster Relief Fund, $400 million in election assistance, an additional $600 per week from the federal government for individuals out of work, and $377 billion for the PPP and EIDA loan programs.

The Paycheck Protection Program and Healthcare Enhancement Act (H.R. 266)

This legislation was signed into law on April 24, 2020 and provided an additional $370 billion to the PPP program, $75 billion for hospitals (along with $100 billion in CARES Act funding), and $25 billion for virus testing.

The Consolidated Appropriations Act (H.R. 133)

This legislation, signed into law on December 29, 2020, provided $900 billion in coronavirus stimulus funding with another round of the Paycheck Protection Program for small businesses, additional unemployment benefits of $300 per week, and $69 billion for vaccine distribution and testing. The bill also included funding for nutrition assistance, childcare, and rental assistance. This bill extended the deadline for counties to spend money allocated through the Coronavirus Relief Fund (CRF) until December 31, 2021.

The American Rescue Plan Act of 2021 (H.R. 1319)

This $1.9 trillion federal stimulus package, signed into law on March 11, 2021, included $350 billion in emergency funding for state, local and territorial governments, including $65 billion for counties. The measure, championed by Senate Majority Leader Charles Schumer, provided $2.2 billion for New York's counties and more than $4 billion for New York City. The measure also provided an additional enhancement to the Federal Medicaid Assistance Percentage (FMAP), $220 billion for schools and universities, $96 billion for public health, $50 billion to help small businesses, and $790 billion to support individual Americans, through extended unemployment insurance benefits, income tax credits, and up to $1,400 in payments to individuals based on income.

Appendix B

Executive Orders

Governor Andrew Cuomo enacted over one hundred executive orders that amended scores of state and local laws, rules, and regulations to address the public health emergency. These EO's carried the same weight as any law enacted by the State Legislature, but only on a temporary basis during the declared pandemic state of emergency.

Executive Order (EO) 202: Declaring a Disaster Emergency in the State of New York

Executive Order (EO) 202.01: Expanding Health Care Options, Changing Public Meeting Laws, and Limiting Large Gathering and Business Capacity

This EO required hospitals to expand the numbers of beds and services, allowed the construction of temporary hospitals, and permitted clinical laboratories to operate temporary collecting stations for COVID-19 test results. The EO also allowed health screenings to be conducted by telephone, and court proceedings to take place electronically. It suspended in-person public meetings and allowed for the attendance of those meetings by telephone or other electronic means. It cancelled all gatherings of more than 500 people and limited any place of business to operate with 50 percent occupancy.

EO 202.02: Allowing No-Excuse Absentee Ballot Voting

EO 202.02 allowed for the electronic application for absentee ballots and reduced the number of signatures on petitions required to run for office pursuant to Section 6-136 of NYS Election Law to 1.5 percent of the enrolled voters required or 30 percent of the stated threshold, whichever is less.

EO 202.03: Canceling Large Events and Limiting the Power of Local Governments

This EO prohibited concerts, conferences, worship services, and performances before audiences of more than fifty persons. It forced all restaurants and bars to stop in-person food and beverage services, and closed casinos, gyms, fitness centers, and movie theaters. The order also prohibited any local government or political subdivision from issuing a local emergency order or declaration of emergency that was inconsistent with—or conflicted with—any of the governor's executive orders.

EO 202.04: Closing Schools, Postponing Elections, and Determining Essential Local Government Employees

This EO required local governments to send home all "nonessential personnel" as determined by the local government, to be able to work from home or take leave without charging accruals, except for those personnel essential to the locality's response to the COVID-19 emergency. Such nonessential personnel were required to total no less than 50 percent of the total number of employees across the entire workforce of such local government or political subdivision. The EO also required the closure of schools across the state. Additionally, any village election was postponed and any elected official holding such position would remain in office until such time as a new election was held.

EO 202.05: Ending Unilateral Local Government EO Power, Closing Indoor Gathering Places, and Suspending Laws to Allow for Medical Services

This EO stated that no local government could issue any local emergency, executive order, or local law with respect to virus response without approval of State Department of Health. A county could close a county-owned public library, but it would need the State Department of Health's permission to close noncounty-owned libraries.

Separately, this EO also closed many common business spaces that hosted large gatherings. This included all indoor portions of retail shopping malls with an excess of one hundred thousand square feet, as well as "places of public amusement," namely amusement rides, carnivals, amusement parks, water parks, aquariums, zoos, arcades, fairs, children's play centers, funplexes, theme parks, bowling alleys, and family and children's attractions. Additionally, this EO suspended various sections of the law to make it easier for the state to add health resources or to shift health policies when needed. This included, allowing physicians, physician assistants, and nurses licensed in other states to practice in New York; and allowing temporary facilities to waive building codes, capacity regulations, and zoning codes.

EO 202.06: Reducing In-person Private Workforce and Giving Approval to the Empire State Development Corporation

This EO reduced the entire New York private in-person workforce by 50 percent. The EO did permit in-person businesses that provided "essential" functions to continue working. Essential businesses were defined as healthcare operations including research and laboratory services; infrastructure (utilities, telecom, airports, and transportation); some manufacturing (food processing and pharmaceuticals); some retail (including grocery and pharmacies); services (including trash collection, mail, shipping, logistics and technology support, and childcare), news media; banks and financial institutions; providers of basic necessities to economically disadvantaged populations; and construction, which would be restricted later. Any other business to be designated as "essential" had to apply to the Empire State Development Corporation for approval.

EO 202.07: Reducing In-Person Employment and Closing More "Public Gathering" Businesses

This EO reduced in-person business density restrictions to 25 percent. The order closed all "personal care" services, including barbershops, hair salons, tattoo or piercing parlors, nail technicians, cosmetologists, estheticians, the provision of electrolysis, and laser hair removal.

EO 202.8: Closing Courts, DMVs, to In-Person Services

This EO limited court operations to essential matters, stating any "commencement, filing, or service of any legal action, notice, motion, or other process or proceeding, as prescribed by the procedural laws of the state, including but not limited to the criminal procedure law, the family court act, the civil practice law and rules, the court of claims act, the surrogate's court procedure act, and the uniform court acts, or by any other statute, local law, ordinance, order, rule, or regulation is hereby tolled." The EO ended all in-person DMV operations. County DMV's could still process car sales but those had to be done by mail or drop box.

Other important actions included private nonessential businesses could no longer have in-person employees; and "(a)ny business violating the above order shall be subject to enforcement as if this were a violation of an order pursuant to Section 12 of the Public Health Law." This was significant because it is informing the public that this and all EOs are not just guidance, they are the law with penalties for violators. Section 12 and 12b of Public Health Law allow for serious civil and even criminal (12b) penalties. Finally, this EO stated that there shall be no enforcement of either an eviction of any tenant residential or commercial or a foreclosure of any residential or commercial property for a period of ninety days.

EO 202.10: Expanding Health Services and Hospitals, Ending Gatherings

This EO required hospitals, surgery centers, office-based surgery practices, and diagnostic and treatment centers to increase beds available with the commissioner being empowered to revoke the operating certificate of any hospital that fails to comply. The EO banned any nonessential gatherings of any size for any reason. This restriction also fell under the Section 12 and Section 12b of Public Health Law, and quickly became one of the hardest issues to enforce. This was because even defining the term "gathering" was difficult. Later this became even more of a challenge when civil unrest in the form of protests became a common occurrence.

EO 202.11: Ending All In-Person Instruction in Schools

This EO closed all in-person learning by requiring schools to be closed until April 15, which was later extended to the rest of the school year.

EO 202.12 and 202.13: Reforming Elections

This EO modified the Election Law to extend the time for mailing annual check of registrants and notice by mail. The extension length would be determined by the New York State Board of Elections. It also postponed the presidential primary and all special elections until June 23, 2020; the circulation, filing, and collection of designation petitions or independent nominating petitioners for any office commencing March 31, 2020, were postponed indefinitely. School board, library board, or village elections were postponed until June 1, 2020.

EO 202.14: Expanding Healthcare Oversight, Requiring Social Distancing

This EO expanded healthcare service ability and oversight. It allowed any medical student graduating in 2020 to practice medicine under supervision if they have been accepted to a residency program within or outside the state. The EO required hospitals and healthcare facilities to inventory and report all PPE, ventilators, respirators, bi-pap, anesthesia, and other "necessary equipment or supplies." The State Department of Health could shift such items not currently needed to a facility in urgent need of that equipment. The public gathering ban was continued with the understanding that people could not gather within six feet and that violations of social distancing were punishable by up to a $1,000 fine.

EO 202.15: Delaying Public Hearings, Enacting More Election Reforms

This EO required public hearings scheduled to take place in April or May of 2020 to be postponed until June 1, 2020. Counties were allowed to continue to livestream public hearings and meetings over the internet. The EO also modified election law to allow absentee ballots to be granted based on temporary illness or "potential for contraction of the COVID-19 virus" for any election held on or before June 23, 2020 and allowed for electronic application for an absentee ballot with no in-person signature or appearance.

EO 202.16: Requiring Private Businesses to Provide Masks

This EO required all essential businesses to provide in-person employees with face coverings at their own expense. Compliance was to be enforced by local law enforcement as a violation of 12 or 12b of the Public Health Law.

EO 202.17: Masking Up Everyone

This EO required any individual who is over age two and able to medically tolerate a face-covering to cover their nose and mouth with a mask or cloth face-covering when in a public place and unable to maintain, or when not maintaining, social distance. Noncompliance was a Public Health Law violation.

EO 202.20 and 202.21: Allowing Online Marriages

This EO waived the sixty-day marriage license requirement, and allowed weddings to be performed remotely, or via audio-visual technology if (1) the couple presented valid photo ID; (2) the video conference allowed interaction between the couple and the clerk; (3) the couple affirmed they are physically in the jurisdiction; (4) the couple faxed or emailed a legible copy of the signed marriage documents to the clerk and witnesses; and (5) the clerk and witnesses could sign the document and transmit it back electronically.

Also, any officiant, public or private, could marry people using the remote system.

EO 202.23: Enacting Nursing Homes Directives, More Election Delays

This EO authorized the commissioner of health to suspend or revoke the operating certificate of any skilled nursing facility or adult care facility if it was determined that such facility did not adhere to any regulations or directives issued by the commissioner and determined not to be in compliance notwithstanding any law to the contrary. The commissioner could appoint a receiver to continue the operations on twenty-four hours' notice to the current operator. The EO also canceled the State Assembly and Senate special elections that were scheduled for June 23, 2020.

EO 202.25: Allowing for Elective Surgeries in Hospitals

This EO allowed general hospitals to perform elective surgeries and procedures so long as, within a county, the total available inpatient capacity was over 30 percent and total ICU available capacity was over 30 percent and the total change in COVID-19 hospitalizations was fewer than ten people. It required hospitals to report the number and type of surgeries.

EO 202.26: Allowing Mail-In Ballots for Elections

This EO authorized the board of elections to obtain absentee ballot applications, ballots, envelopes, postage, and other supplies needed to send out absentee ballots without bidding process in order to allow for voting by absentee ballot. Village elections were rescheduled for September 15, 2020, and absentee ballots for a primary or special election on June 23, 2020 would be provided with a postage-paid return envelope.

EO 202.28: Suspending Evictions and Foreclosures

This EO suspended all evictions and foreclosures where the person is either (1) eligible for unemployment insurance or (2) facing financial hardship due to the COVID-19 pandemic. The EO closed schools for the rest of the academic year.

EO 202.29: Extending Child Victims Act Statute of Limitations

This EO extended the Child Victim's Act window for claims to be filed. The new statute of limitations for CVA claims became January 14, 2021.

EO 202.30: Halting Hospital to Nursing Home Transfers

This EO required all nursing homes to test personnel, contract staff, medical staff, operators, and administrators twice per week. Any staff who refused to be tested were prohibited from providing services to the facility. The EO also prohibited hospitals from discharging any patients to a nursing home unless the nursing home had first certified it was able to care for such patients. Hospitals had to test patients for COVID-19 and could only transfer COVID-negative patients to nursing homes.

EO 202.32: Limiting Gatherings of 10 or More

This EO authorized gatherings of ten or fewer people only for religious services and ceremonies or Memorial Day services. The EO also gave guidance for drive-in or remote religious services to continue in excess of the ten-person limit as long as there was no in-person contact or caravans.

EO 202.33: Enacting Gathering Restrictions to 10 or Less

This EO allowed for ten people or fewer to gather for any reason. The new standard for enforcement was any gathering over ten people.

EO 202.36: Allowing Some Businesses to Reopen

This EO empowered Empire State Development to commence Phase 2 of the economic reopening in certain regions. This allowed barbershops and hair salons to reopen. Auto racetracks could reopen beginning June 3, provided only essential personnel or participants were on the premises, and no visitors or spectators were permitted to be present.

EO 202.38: Opening Restaurants and Bars for Outdoor Service, Allowing Church Gatherings

This EO allowed restaurants and bars to serve customers, but only outside. Restaurants and bars could permit services that complied with other EO restrictions such as gathering limitations, social distancing, and mask wearing. The EO expanded the amount of people that could attend a religious ceremony in areas in Phase 2 to allow for a 25 percent indoor capacity.

EO 202.41: Allowing More Businesses to Reopen

This EO allowed for Phase 3 openings in certain regions. Phase 3 businesses included personal care services such as tattoo and piercing parlors; appearance enhancement practices; massage therapy practices; spas; cosmetology salons; nail salons; tanning salons; and waxing salons.

EO 202.42: Allowing Gatherings to Grow

This EO allowed social gatherings of up to twenty-five people, again with social distancing requirements, in Phase 3 areas.

EO 202.43: Opening County DMVs

This EO allowed county-operated DMV sites to operate, but only by appointment.

EO 202.45: Expanding Gathering Limits Again; Phase 4 Reopen

This EO allowed Phase 4 reopening in certain regions. These businesses included higher education; Pre-K through twelfth grade; arts and entertainment; media production; sports competitions with no fans; malls; gyms; and fitness centers. These businesses had to comply with social distancing, wearing masks, and limited gatherings called for in other executive orders, and required air circulation filters and cleaning protocols. The gathering limit in Phase 4 areas increased to fifty.

EO 202.47: Enforcing Bar Activity, Increasing Criminal Court Functions

This EO allowed peace officers to enforce provisions of the Alcoholic Beverage Control ABC and Public Health laws and/or enforce executive orders. Previously that authority was reserved to others. The EO allowed for in-person criminal appearances, with defendant permission, electronic/remote pleas and appearance virtually with counsel before the grand jury.

EO 202.52: Requiring Bars to Serve Food with Alcohol

This EO required bars and restaurants to serve alcoholic beverages for on- or off-premises consumption only if accompanied by a sold food item.

EO 202.68: Establishing Fines for Gatherings or Violating Social Distancing Rules; Creating COVID-19 Cluster Zones

This EO established a civil penalty of up to $15,000 per day for anyone who encouraged, promoted, or organized a nonessential gathering; authorized local government officials to assess a civil penalty of up to $1,000 for violations of social distancing and face-covering rules; and created zones of "cluster-based cases of COVID-19 at a level that compromises the State's containment of the virus."

EO 202.69: Requiring Automobile Inspections Again, Withholding State Aid to Schools

This EO reinstated the requirement that all cars must be inspected for safety and emissions beginning November 3, 2020. The EO authorized the state director of the budget to withhold funds from schools of local governments if they were found to be in violation of EO 202.68 or any orders issued by the department of health pursuant to EO 202.68.

EO 202.73: Extending More Nursing Home Protections

This EO extended the prior staff testing requirement for nursing homes, but now required that nursing homes within red, orange, or yellow zones to test personnel more frequently for COVID-19.

EO 202.74: Enacting New Restrictions as Positive Numbers Climb

This EO placed a curfew on all bars, liquor stores, restaurants, and gyms. Liquor stores and wine stores had to cease sales and close before 10 p.m..; and could not reopen before "county opening hours permit." Gyms and fitness centers also had to close by 10 p.m.

EO 202.77: Limiting Thanksgiving Gatherings

This EO established a ten-person gathering rule to control the size of in-home gatherings for the Thanksgiving holiday. The EO authorized the health commissioner to change guidelines for accepting patients back to nursing homes from the hospital.

EO 202.79: Allowing Schools Flexibility to Remain Open

This EO extended all prior NY PAUSE orders but allowed for schools within red and orange zones to conduct in-person instruction subject to department of health guidance. The EO allowed hospitals to transfer and allow inter- or intra-system patient load balancing, subject to specific regulations from the commissioner of health.

EO 202.81: Providing More Flexibility for Some Businesses, Less for Others

This EO established that hospitals could discharge COVID-positive patients who have not yet tested negative to nursing homes, provided they are beyond the "infectious period" under CDC policy, but only to a COVID-positive nursing home and if the facility could properly care for the person. The EO closed indoor dining in New York City. Across the state, in orange zones, gyms and fitness centers could open at 25 percent capacity. Barbershops, spas, hair salons, tattoo parlors, nail salons, cosmetologists, estheticians, and all other personal care services could remain open with weekly employee testing.

EO 202.82: Determining Who Could Administer and Receive Vaccines

This EO authorized non-nursing staff, pharmacists, midwives, dentists, podiatrists, EMTs, AEMTs, paramedics, and medical and nursing students to administer the vaccine. The EO authorized the State Department of Health to prioritize who could receive the vaccine and from where.

EO 202.86 through 202.88: Setting Fines for Skipping the Vaccine Priority List

These EOs allowed for the Department of Health to assess civil penalties to any unauthorized entity issuing vaccines. This required the entity to collect information from individuals receiving the vaccine and have them attest to being a member of a priority group. If they failed to do so and/or knowingly issued to someone not a member of a priority group, the entity was subject to a penalty of up to $1 million per dose and/or the loss of its state-issued license. These EOs also required that any entity that receives vaccines to distribute must notify the DOH on the fifth day after receipt if it did not think it would be able to use all the doses. Failure to follow this protocol would result in a $100,000 fine or the elimination of future vaccine allocations.

EO 202.91: Defining the County Government Vaccination Role

This EO required that counties only vaccinate essential workers with their allocation of vaccine and not use this on the general public. Essential workers included but were not limited to first responders and teachers.

EO 202.95 and 202.96: Who Has Been Vaccinated?

These EOs were intended to give the state data regarding vaccinated teachers in order for the state to make more informed schooling determinations. 202.95 required teachers to report to their district if they received a COVID-19 vaccine and for the district to then report weekly to the DOH the percentage of teachers that had been vaccinated. A few days later, the state adjusted this process with 202.96, requiring local health departments to collect and send such data to the DOH.

Appendix C

Sample County Leaders Meeting Agendas

County leaders meetings were part fireside chat and part updates on state executive orders and activities, mixed in with urgent requests for county officials to weigh in on the state budget and additional federal stimulus negotiations. These meetings became the platform through which county leaders could trade ideas on securing PPE; brainstorm ways to shift internal resources and save money; and discuss how counties were managing contact tracing, testing, and helping businesses survive the economic shutdown.

The meetings were moderated by NYSAC Executive Director Stephen Acquario, who typically started with a motivational leadership anecdote. The agenda included: 1. new Association COVID-19 resources; 2. an update on new positive cases and hospitalizations; 3. an update on new state executive orders and announcements by Governor Andrew Cuomo; 4. a discussion of federal activities; and 5. an opportunity for the county leaders to ask questions or make comments. Some meetings included a guest speaker who provided specific information or examples of best COVID-fighting practices.

Below is the text for an internal agenda that staff created for a county leaders meeting.

NYSAC County Leaders Conference Call

Wednesday, March 25, 2020, 7 – 8:30 p.m.

Call agenda:
NYSAC/Local update
COVID-19 status update
State update
Federal update
Q&A

1. NYSAC/Local Update

As your Association, we continue to do everything we can to support your efforts at the local level. Our plan is to continue these calls tomorrow and then pick it up again next Monday – Thursday. We will not be holding these calls Friday, Saturday, or Sunday night this weekend. We want to be able to provide everyone with a state and federal budget update next week as we learn more information.

1a. NYSAC Updates

Take 5 NY

NYSAC is working with a group developing a campaign that county officials can deploy locally to encourage residents to take just five minutes out of each day to call, text, Facetime, or Skype with a friend, loved one, or acquaintance who may be alone during this period of social distancing.

The stress and loneliness associated with social

distancing is real, and this is one way that we can help break down some of that stress and let our friends, neighbors, and loved ones know that they are being remembered and thought of during this time.

The Take 5 NY campaign will help you spread the word locally that your residents can easily take five minutes during the day to check on their friends and neighbors who may be feeling very isolated during these times. We will work with this group to create the messaging and then we will begin deploying this to members tomorrow or Friday.

Financially Difficult Times

We recognize that our counties and local governments are all looking at some dire fiscal times. The primary pressure point for counties—and all local governments—is the level of reserves, the reliance on sales tax as a share of their local revenues, and then the dependence on industries most impacted by the current shutdown (tourism, lodging, restaurants, personal services, nonessential retail, etc.).

Today we posted a new blog called Managing County Finances in the Wake of COVID-19. That blog can be accessed from the top of our health webpage devoted to coronavirus resources. It covers the importance of tracking your COVID-19 expenses, cash management, liquidity analysis, staff shifting, property tax collection, and using a procurement card to make purchases. We will keep working on these issues to do what we can to analyze our environment and provide support and advocacy efforts to help counties through these times.

IBM Watson Call Assistant for County Call Centers

Tomorrow night we will have an IBM partner on the call to talk about a CHAT-BOT (Citizen Support Virtual Agent) that can help county COVID-19 call centers deal with the high volume of incoming calls. The chatbot would overlay your existing website Q&A section or call center and help answer or direct up to 50 percent of the questions from the public. We will hear more about this from IBM tomorrow during our call. If your county is interested but you can't make the call, let us know, and we will connect you to them. Or you can reach out directly to IBM directly by contacting David Sodergren.

2. COVID-19 Status Update

- As of 11:20 a.m. today (3/25), New York State has 30,811 total positive test results. This is an increase of 5,146 from yesterday. Of the 30,811 total positive results, 3,805 are hospitalized (12 percent). Of the 3,805 that are hospitalized, 888 are in the ICU. This means that 3 percent of the positives are in ICU and 23 percent are being hospitalized.
- To date, NYS has tested 103,479 individuals, 13,000 more tests since yesterday.
- There are 285 deaths from COVID-19 in NYS.

Of the positives:

- 17,856 in New York City (represents 58 percent of the total cases in NYS)
- 4,691 in Westchester County
- 3,285 in Nassau County
- 2,260 in Suffolk County
- 968 in Rockland County
- 638 in Orange County
- 153 in Dutchess County
- 152 in Albany County
- 122 in Erie County
- 118 in Monroe County

2a. New York State Update

- Governor Cuomo said today that he has signed off on New York City's plan to reduce density. That plan includes opening streets to foot traffic, reducing density on playgrounds, and prohibiting contact sports. No more basketball in the NYC parks.
    - o The governor doesn't want to close playgrounds but said he will if he has to.
- Some good news today in the press conference: evidence suggests the density control plan is working, at least in terms of the numbers (or percentages) of hospitalizations.
    - o On Sunday, hospitalizations were doubling every 2 days.

- On Monday, that had slowed to doubling every 3 to 4 days.
- On Tuesday, the numbers of hospitalizations were doubling every 4.7 days.

- Apex of need could be in approx. 21 days.
  - The state still needs to ramp up hospital capacity, beds, staff, and equipment (ventilators) for that apex.
- Beds
  - NYS needs 140,000 beds, has 53,000.
  - Hospitals must increase capacity by a minimum of 50 percent with a goal of 100 percent.
- PPE
  - According to the governor, "Right now, and for the foreseeable future, we have a supply so no doctor can say they don't have PPE."
  - He is saying that the state stockpile has the resources.
- Ventilators – In terms of ventilators, the state has:
  - Purchased 7,000+ and they are still shopping for others;
  - The federal government has sent 4,000 ventilators;
  - And the state is studying the "splitting" of ventilators (as Italy did);
  - The governor is still working with the federal gov't to find more ventilators.
- Staff – In response to the call for a healthcare worker reserve, the state has:

- Created a surge healthcare force (retirees, others) - 40,000 responses,
- 6,175 mental health professionals signed up to provide free counseling. The state hotline for mental health counseling is 1-844-863-9314. You may want to reference this on your county's COVID-19 resources.

Federal government

- Working with White House to find ventilators.
- Governor Cuomo asking for "rolling deployment" to help NYS.
  - Apex is sequential (not every state will have a surge at the same time)
  - Cuomo is offering to personally manage redeployment and technical assistance.
- The governor said today that the $2 trillion Senate Stimulus bill would be "terrible" for New York.
  - He said that it would only provide NYS $3.8 billion (out of a $2 trillion package).
  - And it will only provide NYC with $1.3 billion.
  - Meanwhile, we are now the epicenter of this global pandemic. The virus response has already probably cost NYS $1 billion – it will ultimately cost several billion.
- 28 percent of all testing nationwide has been performed by NYS.

    - Any hospital can get a person tested.
    - Strategically we are testing in the densest areas.
    - We have successfully and dramatically slowed the increase in Westchester.
- Ventilators are being put in a stockpile and deployed on an as needed basis.
- After 7 days of being positive, as long as you are 72 hours without symptoms, you can go back to work.
- There is a "risk stratification quotient." We can restart the economy by bringing in younger people who have less risk.
- You should social distance everywhere; you don't need to automatically quarantine for two weeks if you've been to NYC.
- We can't write a budget without additional funding from the federal government.

3b. Utility Providers

PSC approved the postponement of rate increases that were supposed to go into effect on April 1. This will impact two million New Yorkers. New York American Water's rate increases will now go into effect in September. National Grid's increase will go into effect in July.

3c. New NYSDOH Regulations

- Today's state register contains the notice of emergency rulemaking for the emergency regulations adopted by the Public Health and Health Planning Council on March 9, 2020 related to isolation and quarantine.

- These emergency regulations have been in effect since March 9; this is just the formal public notice.
- The regulations:
    - o Further define various terms related to isolation and quarantine;
    - o Expand the state commissioner of health's authority during outbreaks;
    - o Further define roles and responsibilities of local health departments and attending physicians; and
    - o Address civil penalties.
- Your local health departments have received these regulations and they were encouraged to share them with county attorneys as needed.
- Again, these emergency regulations have already been in effect, and this is just the formal public notice.
- The main thing these regulations do is provide the State Department of Health with the authority to take the lead in certain circumstances. Previously, under statute/regs, the local authority had responsibility for isolation and quarantine regulations.
- In a situation like we're in now, it's appropriate for the Department of Health to have that authority as well.

4.Federal Update

4a. COVID-19 Response Efforts

USS *Comfort* (hospital ship) is expected to arrive in New York Harbor on April 7.

- FEMA and HHS are working with New York on additional temporary hospital sites that could be used, including a 600-bed capacity nursing home facility in Brooklyn, and numerous floors of a high-rise building on Wall Street.
- FEMA is working with HHS to deliver additional supplies and ventilators. This includes using its Logistics Supply Chain Management System to procure and track commodities to supplement state and tribal purchases.
- FEMA delivered 400 ventilators to New York on March 23; another 4,000 will be delivered within the next 12 to 24 hours.

<u>How the General Public Can Help</u>

- Cash donations to the nonprofit of your choice is the best donation. Do not collect or distribute donations of supplies without understanding community needs.
- Businesses that have medical supplies or equipment to donate are asked to go to www.fema.gov and provide the offer through our online medical supplies

and equipment form. The direct web link is www.fema.gov/coronavirus/covid-19-donations.

- To sell medical supplies or equipment to the federal government, please email specifics to covidsupplies@fema.dhs.gov.
- Licensed medical volunteers can offer their services by registering with the Emergency System for Advance Registration of Volunteer Health Professionals. You can access a direct link to do so through fema.gov
- One thing people can do to help is to donate blood. Many blood drives have been canceled, impacting the supply. Blood donation centers have the highest standards of safety and infection control. To find where you can donate blood, visit redcross.org.

SNS Update

- The Strategic National Stockpile (SNS) continues to ship medical equipment nationwide.
- As of March 23, the SNS has delivered the following personal protective equipment and supplies to support public health authorities in the state's four largest metro areas and U.S. territories:
  - 7.6 million N95 respirators
  - 14.3 million surgical/face masks
  - 2.4 million face shields
  - 720 ventilators
  - 1.9 million gowns

- o 8,500 coveralls
- o 12.4 million gloves
- Additionally, FEMA purchased and delivered:
  - o 414,000 N95 respirator masks
  - o More than 550 bottles of hand sanitizer
  - o 1.1 million gloves
  - o More than 4,000 cases of disposable garments
  - o 1,500 Tyvek suits

4b. President Trump Press Conference (6 p.m. 3/25)

Considering an executive order to ban the export of medical equipment from the United States. Within three weeks of the bill being signed, the White House expects checks to be sent in the mail to Americans.

4c. Third Economic Stimulus Package

Early this morning, the Senate and White House reached a bipartisan agreement on a third stimulus package. This package is a sweeping $1.7 trillion bill to help fight the COVID-19 pandemic and then jump start the economy.

Senator Schumer and Senator Gillibrand were able to provide a summary of the legislation. At this point, this legislation is a framework for an agreement. The timeline for this legislation to be passed remains unknown at this time. Some of the legislative proposals contained within the package, include:

- **$150 billion state and local government stimulus program.** Of this allocation, at least $5.8 billion will be directed to New York, and with more than a $1.4 billion going to New York City and about half-a-billion to Long Island.
- **$260 billion unemployment insurance expansion program.** The plan will deliver at least $15 billion directly to New York. Payments of $1,200 for individuals and $2,400 for couples account for another $15.5 billion to New York.
- **$150 billion for a new program to provide direct aid to health care institutions** on the front line of this crisis—hospitals, public entities, not-for profit entities, and Medicare and Medicaid enrolled suppliers and institutional providers—to cover costs related to this public health crisis.
- **$16 billion to replenish the Strategic National Stockpile** supplies of pharmaceuticals, personal protective equipment, and other medical supplies, which are distributed to state and local health agencies, hospitals and other healthcare entities facing shortages during emergencies.
- **$4.3 billion to support federal, state, and local public health agencies** to prevent, prepare for, and respond to the coronavirus, including for the purchase of personal protective equipment; laboratory testing to detect positive cases; infection control and mitigation at the local level to prevent the spread of the virus;

and other public health preparedness and response activities.

- **$200 million for CMS to assist nursing homes** with infection control and support states' efforts to prevent the spread of coronavirus in nursing homes.
- **$45 billion for FEMA's Disaster Relief Fund** to provide for the immediate needs of state, local, tribal, and territorial governments to protect citizens and help them recover from the overwhelming effects of COVID-19. Reimbursable activities may include medical response, personal protective equipment, National Guard deployment, coordination of logistics, safety measures, and community services nationwide
- **$400 million for FEMA grants, including**:
  - o $100 million Assistance to Firefighter Grants to provide personal protective equipment, supplies, and reimbursements
  - o $100 million for Emergency Management Performance Grants which focus on emergency preparedness
  - o $200 million for the Emergency Food and Shelter Program which provides shelter, food, and supportive services through local service organizations
- More than $7 billion for affordable housing and homelessness assistance programs. This funding will help low-income and working-class Americans avoid evictions and minimize any impacts caused by loss of employment, and childcare, or other unforeseen

circumstances related to COVID-19, and support additional assistance to prevent eviction and for people experiencing homelessness.

- **$25 billion in aid to our nation's transit systems** to help protect public health and safety while ensuring access to jobs, medical treatment, food, and other essential services. $25 billion allocation for transit, delivering $4.35 billon to the New York, $3.8 billion of that exclusively for MTA.
- **$15.85 billion for to help our nation's veterans**, including to help treat COVID-19, purchase test kits and procure personal protective equipment for clinicians, and $590 million in dedicated funding to treat vulnerable veterans, including homeless veterans and those in VA-run nursing homes.
- **$850 million in Byrne-JAG grants** for state and local law enforcement and jails to purchase personal protective equipment, medical supplies, and overtime.
- **$425 million to increase access to mental health services in communities.**
- **$400 million in election assistance** for the states to help prepare for the 2020 election cycle, including to increase the ability to vote by mail, expand early voting and online registration, and increase the safety of voting in person by providing additional voting facilities and more poll workers.
- **Emergency appropriations totaling $180 billion** that range from billions for hard-hit

airports, expanded benefits to SNAP, funding for childcare, of which New York would receive an additional $162 million, nutrition for seniors, and nearly $1 billion to help heat homes when income becomes a problem.

5. Q&A

Roll call of the counties.

Appendix D

Positive COVID Cases by County by Month

County	3/15/2020	4/15/2020	5/15/2020	6/15/2020	7/15/2020	8/15/2020	9/15/2020	10/15/2020	11/15/2020	12/15/2020	1/15/2021	2/15/2020	3/15/2021
Albany	12	581	1,572	2,026	2,290	2,654	2,948	3,383	4,572	8,405	15,771	20,090	21,688
Allegany	2	28	44	55	70	80	94	188	650	1,451	2,313	2,768	2,962
Bronx	57	25,932	42,812	46,710	48,575	50,724	52,371	54,198	58,905	73,010	99,030	129,691	148,599
Broome	1	167	413	656	861	1,166	1,428	2,784	4,431	6,692	10,743	13,803	15,883
Cattaraugus	0	32	65	107	142	171	245	393	683	1,868	3,308	4,185	4,589
Cayuga	0	36	63	106	128	164	193	275	639	1,697	4,267	5,182	5,493
Chautauqua	0	24	48	108	191	263	527	771	1,248	2,458	5,350	7,058	7,582
Chemung	0	70	134	138	151	189	275	1,156	2,380	3,848	5,479	6,307	6,568
Chenango	0	73	115	139	178	218	245	294	506	917	1,680	2,328	2,585
Clinton	0	46	91	99	111	132	154	190	380	731	2,040	3,258	3,914
Columbia	0	99	338	442	489	552	577	635	886	1,258	2,344	3,251	3,522
Cortland	0	24	34	42	63	97	137	387	771	1,561	2,587	3,027	3,309
Delaware	1	47	68	88	92	107	129	157	280	534	983	1,385	1,710
Dutchess	10	2,085	3,527	4,075	4,357	4,686	5,014	5,305	6,224	9,642	16,115	21,024	24,039
Erie	6	1,850	4,867	6,852	7,927	9,147	10,752	12,468	18,018	34,181	50,716	62,208	68,746
Essex	0	12	32	40	51	59	154	184	231	402	952	1,249	1,399
Franklin	0	13	18	25	38	54	63	75	189	485	1,086	1,838	2,222
Fulton	0	25	148	236	266	303	325	357	401	921	1,999	3,072	3,547
Genesee	0	78	178	213	254	285	307	371	615	1,721	3,566	4,204	4,593
Greene	2	74	211	252	271	298	318	464	587	914	1,964	2,539	2,786
Hamilton	0	3	5	6	6	11	14	16	26	73	145	271	290
Herkimer	1	43	91	128	202	283	314	367	504	1,279	3,485	4,460	4,655
Jefferson	0	48	71	81	102	143	158	186	332	1,121	3,031	4,494	5,042
Kings	84	33,521	51,991	58,274	61,124	63,861	66,468	72,598	81,686	103,969	147,252	191,275	223,601
Lewis	0	8	13	20	32	47	50	55	247	603	1,419	1,949	2,156
Livingston	0	32	107	123	153	178	197	234	499	1,206	2,605	3,374	3,674
Madison	0	105	258	336	377	421	480	528	727	1,684	3,047	3,710	3,949
Monroe	9	932	2,192	3,402	4,317	5,165	5,809	6,628	10,680	24,946	43,226	50,830	54,377
Montgomery	1	32	75	104	141	187	218	252	325	857	2,123	3,002	3,343
Nassau	107	27,772	39,033	41,290	42,506	43,929	45,906	48,377	54,309	72,904	111,393	140,686	157,985
New York	172	17,091	24,982	27,677	29,516	31,398	32,835	34,735	40,226	53,872	75,212	97,455	113,871
Niagara	0	216	770	1,171	1,364	1,532	1,694	1,938	2,753	6,258	11,664	14,803	15,854

The number of COVID-19 cases per month per county was collected and published by the New York State Department of Health at https://health.data.ny.gov/Health/New-York-State-Statewide-COVID-19-Testing/xdss-u53e.

County	3/15/2020	4/15/2020	5/15/2020	6/15/2020	7/15/2020	8/15/2020	9/15/2020	10/15/2020	11/15/2020	12/15/2020	1/15/2021	2/15/2021	3/15/2021
Oneida	0	249	751	1,301	1,868	2,198	2,359	2,574	3,603	8,368	16,342	19,215	20,262
Onondaga	1	462	1,469	2,545	3,225	3,674	4,133	4,946	7,892	16,054	26,954	31,580	33,249
Ontario	1	65	139	234	317	368	449	549	969	2,203	4,592	5,533	6,045
Orange	11	5,888	9,879	10,580	10,895	11,254	11,711	13,098	15,182	20,114	28,168	34,898	39,795
Orleans	0	34	163	268	288	301	322	359	521	923	1,882	2,373	2,512
Oswego	0	44	83	139	227	271	409	579	987	2,547	4,762	5,798	6,271
Otsego	0	44	67	81	92	118	318	362	466	941	1,600	2,196	2,628
Putnam	2	573	1,127	1,292	1,385	1,461	1,565	1,716	2,186	3,919	6,294	7,943	8,860
Queens	124	37,918	58,841	64,042	66,735	69,174	71,309	74,798	82,775	105,740	149,816	193,929	223,783
Rensselaer	0	137	438	514	639	795	887	1,020	1,333	2,789	6,596	8,621	9,518
Richmond	20	8,684	12,974	13,888	14,417	15,066	15,642	16,605	19,749	29,167	43,368	53,486	60,747
Rockland	13	8,752	12,688	13,460	13,763	14,007	14,660	17,063	19,904	24,555	31,346	36,954	41,175
St. Lawrence	0	93	192	215	237	263	310	353	573	1,409	3,437	5,034	5,806
Saratoga	5	231	423	522	624	792	970	1,190	1,694	3,716	8,839	11,415	12,577
Schenectady	4	245	613	735	896	1,119	1,362	1,485	1,890	4,014	8,347	10,493	11,268
Schoharie	0	20	47	54	62	69	83	100	145	378	873	1,125	1,301
Schuyler	0	6	8	12	15	23	33	85	231	400	699	845	885
Seneca	0	18	50	64	76	93	104	125	214	509	1,177	1,500	1,706
Steuben	0	154	233	257	279	306	334	817	1,434	2,531	4,496	5,368	5,685
Suffolk	63	24,182	37,942	40,738	42,333	44,159	45,843	47,815	53,653	77,681	124,384	155,149	171,950
Sullivan	0	437	1,217	1,433	1,469	1,493	1,561	1,668	1,981	2,510	3,751	4,506	5,055
Tioga	1	27	112	140	163	195	221	413	957	1,407	2,145	2,687	2,947
Tompkins	1	116	138	173	198	238	386	523	811	1,637	2,572	3,340	3,634
Ulster	7	761	1,537	1,742	1,894	2,095	2,229	2,395	2,800	4,547	7,448	9,541	10,842
Warren	0	81	228	257	285	312	351	437	507	775	1,982	2,720	2,991
Washington	0	46	218	243	250	261	286	325	404	606	1,424	2,190	2,482
Wayne	0	49	92	134	223	269	304	373	780	1,790	3,568	4,322	4,637
Westchester	223	21,828	32,097	34,358	35,422	36,453	37,634	39,288	44,576	60,540	82,933	102,197	113,577
Wyoming	1	34	78	93	103	118	130	160	354	939	2,075	2,712	2,963
Yates	0	7	22	40	50	59	62	81	209	378	783	1,001	1,037

Appendix E

COVID-19 Deaths by County by Month

County	3/15/2020	4/15/2020	5/15/2020	6/15/2020	7/15/2020	8/15/2020	9/15/2020	10/15/2020	11/15/2020	12/15/2020	1/15/2021	2/15/2021	3/15/2021
Albany	0	22	86	106	109	118	123	124	135	173	248	320	339
Allegany	0	1	2	2	2	2	2	5	35	65	75	80	82
Bronx	0	2052	4192	4604	4805	4879	4934	4973	5020	5062	5243	5657	6089
Broome	0	6	34	56	64	78	85	87	123	178	248	322	341
Cattaraugus	0	0	2	6	6	6	6	14	21	29	60	74	79
Cayuga	0	1	2	2	2	2	2	3	5	14	68	87	90
Chautauqua	0	1	2	3	3	4	4	4	5	11	51	119	129
Chemung	0	2	2	2	2	2	2	7	27	78	107	127	131
Chenango	0	0	3	6	6	6	6	6	7	13	38	64	70
Clinton	0	3	4	4	4	4	5	5	5	5	13	22	29
Columbia	0	10	32	46	47	47	47	47	55	58	66	91	97
Cortland	0	1	1	1	1	1	1	1	1	11	52	60	60
Delaware	0	1	2	3	4	4	4	5	6	7	16	31	34
Dutchess	0	38	120	147	152	153	154	163	174	208	290	397	418
Erie	0	104	400	554	580	601	616	640	694	983	1339	1550	1631
Essex	0	0	0	0	0	0	11	14	14	14	16	26	26
Franklin	0	0	0	0	0	1	1	1	3	9	9	11	12
Fulton	0	2	14	26	26	28	28	28	28	29	47	76	85
Genesee	0	2	4	5	6	6	6	6	6	21	91	118	120
Greene	0	0	9	13	13	13	14	15	16	18	51	67	72
Hamilton	0	0	1	1	1	1	1	1	1	1	1	2	2
Herkimer	0	3	3	3	3	8	10	10	10	14	46	103	107
Jefferson	0	0	0	0	0	1	1	1	1	6	20	60	63
Kings	1	3007	6276	6936	7189	7266	7306	7361	7452	7575	7994	8783	9444
Lewis	0	3	5	5	5	5	5	5	5	11	22	29	31
Livingston	0	1	3	4	4	6	6	6	7	20	36	53	57
Madison	0	2	7	9	9	9	9	9	9	27	75	82	85
Monroe	0	43	145	230	248	255	258	260	269	375	737	954	1005
Montgomery	0	2	4	4	4	4	9	9	11	22	71	97	107
Nassau	0	1057	2027	2167	2191	2195	2200	2205	2231	2304	2518	2824	2987
New York	0	1228	2684	3023	3133	3159	3173	3188	3208	3253	3419	3755	4045
Niagara	0	10	52	83	85	88	89	90	96	141	233	296	323

The deaths per county per month was collected from USAFacts, which partnered with academic institutions like the University of Pennsylvania and Stanford University.

usafacts.org/visualizations/coronavirus-covid-19-spread-map/state/new-york

County	3/15/2020	4/15/2020	5/15/2020	6/15/2020	7/15/2020	8/15/2020	9/15/2020	10/15/2020	11/15/2020	12/15/2020	1/15/2021	2/15/2021	3/15/2021
Oneida	0	3	30	81	109	117	120	126	139	196	331	460	486
Onondaga	0	15	73	155	166	178	180	182	196	288	517	607	645
Ontario	0	1	8	23	27	27	28	28	30	37	77	88	90
Orange	0	133	335	369	404	408	411	416	425	469	562	615	661
Orleans	0	0	22	49	55	55	55	55	56	59	67	80	82
Oswego	0	2	2	2	3	3	3	3	4	20	62	88	89
Otsego	0	2	3	4	4	4	4	4	5	6	21	41	44
Putnam	0	31	56	62	63	63	63	63	64	66	70	84	88
Queens	0	2980	5877	6452	7116	7207	7231	7282	7322	7419	7782	8485	9092
Rensselaer	0	6	23	27	33	39	42	42	45	67	101	123	132
Richmond	0	425	914	1024	1072	1077	1084	1089	1107	1188	1363	1524	1631
Rockland	1	229	468	503	506	507	509	509	518	554	615	674	700
St. Lawrence	0	1	2	3	4	4	4	4	6	27	55	75	92
Saratoga	0	6	13	15	15	15	15	15	17	25	76	141	151
Schenectady	0	12	25	32	36	41	46	48	52	63	116	173	185
Schoharie	0	1	2	2	2	2	2	2	2	2	5	11	13
Schuyler	0	0	0	0	0	0	0	0	3	6	10	11	12
Seneca	0	1	1	1	1	1	1	2	2	14	45	52	55
Steuben	0	9	26	29	29	39	39	66	72	100	130	137	140
Suffolk	0	653	1709	1955	1993	1998	2010	2017	2026	2132	2545	2968	3162
Sullivan	0	7	28	35	36	37	37	37	38	40	48	58	62
Tioga	0	0	16	19	20	21	21	25	44	54	54	56	56
Tompkins	0	0	0	0	0	0	0	0	0	9	22	41	47
Ulster	0	14	64	80	81	81	83	84	87	118	183	221	233
Warren	0	3	25	30	30	30	30	30	30	30	36	53	55
Washington	0	3	14	14	14	14	14	14	14	14	21	49	54
Wayne	0	1	2	2	2	3	3	3	10	28	50	62	65
Westchester	0	640	1269	1405	1436	1447	1453	1463	1488	1575	1774	2027	2149
Wyoming	0	4	4	4	4	4	4	5	5	13	41	48	49
Yates	0	0	4	6	6	6	6	6	6	7	16	26	26

AFTERWORD

It has been over a year since the beginning of the pandemic, and three months since the county executives submitted their final accounts of their response to the pandemic through 2020. Still, the pandemic is not over, with many new milestones continuing to impact how counties are working to address the spread of COVID-19 and help their communities recover from the economic devastation. This timeline follows their activities in 2021 from the beginning of the new presidential administration through the final days of this book's production.

January 20 – In the midst of the COVID pandemic, the Hon. Joseph R. Biden, Sr. was sworn in as our nation's 46th president.

January 20 – New York State designates that individuals 65 years of age and older, as well as frontline workers, were eligible to receive COVID-19 vaccines.

January 28 – New York Attorney General Letitia James releases report on nursing homes' response to COVID-19, revealing that the New York State Department of Health undercounted by nearly 50 percent the actual number of COVID-19 related deaths.

January 28 – Later that afternoon, NYS Health Commissioner Howard Zucker updated the number of COVID-19 related nursing home deaths to include an additional 4,000 dead.

February 10 – A senior aide to the governor told lawmakers that the Executive branch withheld the state's nursing home death toll from the State Legislature and federal government out of fear of a federal investigation.

February 11 – President Biden announced the purchase of an additional 200 million vaccine doses from Pfizer and Moderna. These additional vaccines were on top of the 400 million ordered by the Trump Administration.

February 17 – News reports indicate that the United States Attorney in Brooklyn and the Federal Bureau of Investigations (FBI) began a preliminary investigation into how New York handled data about Covid-19 nursing home deaths.

February 27 – The U.S. Food and Drug Administration issued an emergency use authorization (EUA) for the third vaccine for the prevention of COVID-19. The EUA allows the Janssen/Johnson & Johnson COVID-19 vaccine to be administered to individuals 18 years of age and older.

March 2 – President Biden announced his administration was invoking the Defense Production Act to expand production of the Janssen/Johnson & Johnson COVID-19 vaccine through a historic manufacturing collaboration between two of the largest American health care and pharmaceutical companies, Merck and Johnson & Johnson.

March 4 – The *New York Times* reported that aides to the Governor altered a Department of Health Report published in July to suggest fewer nursing home residents died from COVID-19. According to the *Times*, the state did not count nursing home residents who died after being transferred to a hospital.

March 5 – The New York State Legislature revised the executive powers it had granted the governor one year before.

March 10 – President Biden announced the purchase of an additional 100 million doses of the Janssen/Johnson & Johnson vaccine.

March 10 – New Yorkers 60 years of age and older were now eligible to receive a COVID vaccine.

March 11 – The New York State Assembly opened an impeachment investigation of the Governor for actions taken during the pandemic.

March 11 – President Biden signed the American Rescue Plan Act, championed by Senate Majority Leader Charles Schumer of New York. The $1.9 billion stimulus package included $350 billion for states and local governments, including $65 billion for counties across the nation.

March 13 – According to media reporters, a county executive filed a preliminary ethical complaint with the Attorney General's Public Integrity Bureau after receiving a call from the head of the State's vaccination program to gauge support for the governor.

March 17 – Government employees, nonprofit workers, and essential building service workers became eligible for the COVID-19 vaccine.

March 19 – President Biden announced that 100 million COVID-19 vaccine shots had been distributed. In December, he had pledged to meet this goal in his first 100 days in office. He was able to achieve it 80 days into his administration.

March 23 – New Yorkers 50 years of age and older could sign up to be vaccinated.

March 29 – Dr. Deborah Birx, the coordinator of President Donald J. Trump's Coronavirus Task Force admitted on CNN that the lack of consistent messaging out of the Administration may be to blame for as many as 400,000 deaths in the United States.

March 30 – More than 30 percent of New Yorkers had received at least one vaccine dose.

March 30 – All New Yorkers age 30 or older were now eligible to make appointments for a vaccine.

March 31 – 9.4 million vaccine doses had been administered in New York State, with 30 percent of all New Yorkers receiving at least one dose.

April 5 – 33 percent of all New Yorkers had at least one vaccine dose, and 20 percent were fully vaccinated.

April 6 – Vaccine eligibility was lowered for all New Yorkers age 16 and above.

April 6 — State lawmakers repeal immunity provisions for nursing homes, hospitals, and health care facilities and professionals from liability resulting from treatment of individuals with COVID-19 during the public health emergency.

April 7 – According to the *New York Times*, the number of deaths related to COVID-19 in New York State was 50,200. The governor claimed the number was 40,922.

April 13 – The FDA and CDC instituted a pause in the administration of the Jansen/Johnson & Johnson vaccine to examine cases of a rare blood-clotting disorder that happened to six recipients out of nearly seven million doses dispensed.

April 19 – The New York State Comptroller issued a referral to the New York Attorney General to investigate the use of state resources in the drafting of *An American Crisis*, the book that was published by the governor in October 2020.

April 28, 2021 – The State Legislature passed a concurrent resolution repealing a number of the governor's executive orders, including the requirement that food be sold with the sale of alcoholic beverage sales in bars and restaurants. It also eliminates penalties and prioritization rules that slow down the vaccination process (use it or lose it in 7 days). The resolution also requires individuals who volunteer to take on significant COVID government work will now be treated as Public Officers and must comply with government disclosure and transparency rules. This repealed the executive order that exempted volunteers from the state's ethics rules.

April 29, 2021 – The governor's vaccination czar resigned. He had been a volunteer coordinating the state's ongoing vaccine roll out program.

ACKNOWLEDGMENTS

There are a number of people who helped make this book possible. First and foremost, the county executives whose stories fill many of these pages. This book draws on their experiences as they confronted the pandemic and made a difference in their county. The NYSAC staff proved themselves to be essential in every sense of the word, keeping New York's counties united during the worst public health crisis in modern history. NYSAC staff members Dave Lucas, Patrick Cummings, Alex LaMonte, and Ryan Gregiore have all provided critical contributions to this book.

On behalf of NYSAC and the NYS County Executives Association, we thank all our county leaders for sharing their accounts and everything they learned during this terrible time.

We thank the NYSAC President Hon. John "Jack" Marren from Ontario County, and the entire NYSAC board of directors for their invaluable guidance and support. Jack's contribution here reflects the challenges of running a town and a county during a public health crisis. We thank Hon. Daniel P. McCoy, the president of the NYS County Executives Association, whose swift actions united the county executives during the worst crisis of their lifetime. We thank Hon. Marcus Molinaro of Dutchess County, who became the president of the County Executives' Association in October 2020 and guided the organization with both wisdom and good cheer.

The partnership that NYSAC forged with the county health directors and commissioners during this pandemic was invaluable and should stand the test of time. We appreciate the tireless efforts of the New York State Association of County Health Officials and its President Kevin Watkins, Executive Director Sarah Ravenhall, and Program Directors Cristina Dyer-Drobnack and Robert Viets. They were the tip of the spear in fighting this virus, and their perspective and expertise were consistently professional and reassuring.

We also worked closely throughout this pandemic with the chairs of the legislative bodies, capably led by Hon. John Becker of Madison County; county administrators and managers, adeptly represented by Shaun Groden of Greene County; and the county attorneys, led by Ellen Coccoma of Otsego County, who spent day and night interpreting laws, executive orders, and public health protocols. A special thank you goes out to Greene County Attorney Ed Kaplan, who counseled our Association during the height of the pandemic.

We are also grateful to Dutchess County Commissioner

of Emergency Management Dana Smith and all of the county emergency managers and sheriffs who devoted themselves to running the counties' emergency operations centers that made such a profound difference to their communities. Commissioner Smith is a true professional and public servant and helped to ensure that the county EOCs across the state had the personal protective equipment they needed.

Finally, we would never have been able to chronicle these stories without the generous support of Matthew Chase, executive director of the National Association of Counties. Matt's calm demeanor and solid judgment helped unify the nation at the local government level, and we wish to acknowledge his many contributions to New York's counties through this catastrophe.

Much of the organization and structure of the book is credited to NYSAC Deputy Director Mark LaVigne, who put his shoulder to the wheel to keep this big idea moving from rough draft to publication. We are grateful to author Peter Golden for his contributions, his revisions, and his attention to detail and skill with the English language and for his deep appreciation for county leadership during the COVID-19 pandemic.

[illegible] the world [illegible]

[illegible] through this life [illegible]

[illegible]

ABOUT THE AUTHORS

Stephen Acquario, Esq., is executive director and general counsel of the New York State Association of Counties. In this capacity, he has counseled local government officials on all aspects of governance for the past thirty years. This experience put him in a position to serve county leaders as they faced historic challenges.

Peter Golden is an award-winning journalist, historian, and novelist. His latest novel, *Nothing Is Forgotten,* which explores the connection between the Holocaust and Cold War, is published by Atria Books/Simon & Schuster.

Mark LaVigne, Ph.D., has spent more than twenty-five years in organizational and political communication, working with federal, state and local government officials. He supported county leaders as they communicated with the public during the COVID-19 pandemic.